SELL
your way to the
TOP

SELL your way to the TOP

How YOU can sell more of EVERYTHING

PETER THOMSON

Acknowledgements

Many people have assisted with the production of this book. I am delighted to have the opportunity to thank all of them and in particular:

My wife Sharon, for all her support and positive attitude and for helping to create the time.

My friend Barry Sadler for allowing me to test so many sales ideas on him over so many years.

My secretary Tracey for her hard work and patience.

My four sons James, Richard, Stephen and David for being the victims of all the techniques for so long.

First published in 1993

Kogan Page Limited
120 Pentonville Road
London N1 9JN

British Library Cataloguing in Publication Data

A CIP record for this book is available from the British Library.

ISBN 0 7494 1030 2

Printed and bound in Great Britain by Clays Ltd, St Ives plc

Contents

Preface

Can you imagine a world without sales people? Some people would think a world like that would be wonderful, but given a few years the whole economy would grind to a halt and our incomes would fall through the floor.

Well, we could advertise our products or services in the newspapers, couldn't we . . . but who would sell the newspapers? Who would sell the printing presses on which the newspapers were printed? Who would sell the printing inks?

All of us, regardless of our position, age, sex, colour of collar or job description are in the sales business. From the moment we open our eyes to the time we fall asleep at the end of another successful day we have been . . . selling.

OK, these days it's given such euphemistic names as 'marketing', 'customer service', 'representing' or a variety of others, but it's all selling:

- Mum persuading the kids to tidy their room.
- The union representative negotiating the next pay rise.
- The business owner attempting to get an increased overdraft.
- The sales person selling the company's products.

It's all selling . . . So how are we going to increase our success in selling? How are we going to sell our way to the top?

We need to take from the back of our heads the skills we already possess, dust them off, polish them up, add in some new skills, blend them all together and put them back in the front of our heads so that we remember to use them more often.

The ideas in this book have been tried, have been tested and have been proved successful.

Take the methods that suit you, blend them with your own ideas, constantly review your progress until you have a personal blueprint for success. In that way you cannot help but . . . sell your way to the top.

Peter Thomson
February 1993

Introduction

Before we start exploring the ways we can increase our potential for selling, let me make one thing absolutely clear. I do not have all the answers; I possibly know most of the questions, but your business is your business and we will have to work together to find the answers to the questions we ask. I am sure, like me, you already know most of the skills in selling, but what some of us do, some of the time, is to forget to use those skills. Be honest, I have done it, you have done it; we've come out of meetings and said, 'If only I'd . . . I would have . . .'

There is an expression I heard years ago: the day you stop *learning* is the day you stop *earning*. What happens in a lot of businesses is that people say they have five, ten or even 15 years' experience in selling, when the truth is they have one year's experience, five, ten or 15 times. They've stopped learning, they've become resistant to change.

Let's look at other professions. Imagine you had a dog and the dog was sick and you took him down to the local vet and the vet said to you: 'Since I came out of veterinary school I haven't bothered to learn anything else, anything new. I didn't buy any books or attend any seminars or meetings. I still do the things I always did.' Would you trust that man to cure your dog? I doubt it.

Or can you imagine a situation where someone – John – was to be in court charged with a crime he didn't commit? As he was about to go into court the barrister said to him: 'John, I thought I'd just let you know, since I came out of law school I haven't read any new books or learned anything new, but don't worry, I always just think on my feet. Somehow we'll get through.' Would you entrust your future liberty to that barrister? No, of course not.

This book is not designed to be a one-way street with me just expressing my opinions; after all, opinions are like belly-buttons – everybody has one. So this book will need to be a two-way street: an interchange of ideas and experiences which will lead us to a successful conclusion. As I said, your business is your business so you will need to customise the information discussed here to ensure it is relevant to your business, your use and your style.

Throughout the book there will be a number of quizzes and tests;

their purpose is not to prove anybody right or wrong, but simply to focus our minds on the topics in question. Many of those tests are self-assessment, so please don't compare your marks with those of others. It may be that Jayne thinks she has good abilities in one particular topic and marks herself as eight out of ten. Tim, on the other hand, has exactly the same skill level and marks himself six out of ten. It is *self*-assessment.

As you read this book, make 'key word' or 'key picture' notes. The idea is based on Tony Buzan's belief that the best notes we ever take from any book, seminar meeting or training session are in 'key words' and pictures and preferably in colour.

As Buzan says: 'Can you recall a ten-word sentence from any time in your life?' No, it's difficult, isn't it? But if I said to you, 'Can you picture yourself eating ice cream?', the answer would be yes! Our minds think in pictures, so take colourful 'key word' and 'key picture' notes so it is easier for you to review the information later. If you take your notes in monotone you will end up with monotonous notes, so use as many colours as possible.

At the end of each topic I will discuss the steps that we need to take to improve our abilities in that subject. Again, your notes for the steps need to be in key-word and picture format.

The system I use, if I am trying to remember that I *shouldn't do something*, is to draw a picture and put a large cross over the top of it. If I am trying to remember *to do something* then I will draw the picture and put a large tick at the side. When we have completed all the topics you will have an action pack you can dip into daily to refresh your memory on a particular topic or use as a personal training programme over weeks or months. Or, if you are in sales management, that you could use as a manual for the preparation of a complete sales training course for your team.

It's said that we remember about 5 per cent of what we hear, 25 per cent of what we see and 90 per cent of what we do. Therefore for each subject we discuss make an action plan. They are an essential part of the programme, as it is by constantly acting upon the ideas we hear that we will be able to meet our primary goal. Take out the information we already know, add in some new ideas and put them all back together in the front of our minds so we remember to use them more often.

The review plan is simple to use. When you have decided the last *target* date of your actions, simply write for that day in your diary the word 'Review' and the name of the topic in hand. When that day arrives, go back to your notes and review the actions you have decided to take. You will then know if you are at the level you desire for that particular subject, and if not can decide on further actions to improve your skills.

In order to have a starting point, I would like you to take the self-assessment test. This is a 30-question test and its purpose is to focus our minds on the topics we are going to discuss.

Self-assessment test

One of the major traits of successful people is their ability to be self-analytical. Self-analysis must not be confused with self-criticism. The ability to analyse covers positive as well as negative qualities. Recognising the positive things we do and making sure that we keep doing them. Recognising the areas in which we could improve and taking action to do something positive about that situation.

The self-assessment test over the page has been designed to cover 30 main areas in which we need to have a high degree of skill to be successful in our chosen careers. Give yourself a score for your skill level, out of a maximum of 10 points, in response to each question.

Do the test *three* times:

1. Now, before reading the book. This is your *before* score.
2. After reading the book. This is your *after* score.
3. Readjust your 'before' score to ensure that, with your current knowledge, you have a correct starting position. Sometimes we don't know that we don't know.

You will be able to compare your correct 'before' score with your 'after' score to see how much you have already improved.

Date			
Name	**Before score**		**After score**
1. Do I have good listening skills?			
2. Do I have a positive attitude?			
3. Do I understand why people buy?			
4. Do I have a prepared opening statement?			
5. Do I understand the difference between open and closed questions?			
6. Do I avoid procrastination?			
7. Do I understand the difference between *features* and *benefits*?			
8. Do I always talk to customers in terms of benefits to them?			
9. Am I well presented? (car/briefcase/self)			
10. Do I take notice of my body language?			
11. Do I take notice of other people's body language?			
12. Am I a good communicator?			
13. Do I write letters that produce results?			
14. Am I self-analytical?			
15. Do I analyse my customers?			
16. Do I have high self-esteem?			
17. Do I have high self-confidence?			
18. Am I good at negotiating?			

19. Do I keep accurate records?			
20. Do I have written goals?			
21. Am I good at handling objections?			
22. Do I know how to close a sale?			
23. Do I close often enough?			
24. Am I creative?			
25. Do I keep a diary?			
26. Do I have daily action lists?			
27. Do I take referrals on every possible occasion?			
28. Am I able to handle rejection?			
29. Do I practise my skills every week?			
30. Do I like myself?			

CHAPTER 1

Active listening

We're going to start this topic by having a quiz. Write your answers in the space provided below.

1. ____________________

2. ____________________

3. ____________________

4. ____________________

5. ____________________

6. ____________________

Question 1

You go into a log cabin with one match in a box and in the log cabin is:

- A wood-burning stove
- A candle
- A paraffin lamp.

Which do you light first for *maximum warmth*?

Question 2

In Scotland, is a man allowed by law to marry his widow's sister?

Question 3

How many of each *species* did Moses take into the Ark?

Question 4

Some months have 31 days, some have 30 days. How many have 28 days?

Question 5

Guy Fawkes, bonfire night, gunpowder plot and all that; do they have a 5th of November in America?

Question 6

A plane is flying over Europe and crashes on the border of France and Germany. One-third of the plane is in France, two-thirds of the plane is in Germany. In which country do they bury the survivors – France or Germany?

OK, that's the end of the test. Now we'll do the marking. Here are the answers:

Question 1, the log cabin, which do you light first for maximum warmth? Who put the wood-burning stove?, who put the candle? who put the paraffin lamp? No! None of the those is right, the correct answer is . . . the match. Score one point.

Question 2, the man in Scotland, is he allowed by law to marry his widow's sister? Who said yes? Who said no? Do you know why you said no? Well, if she's his widow then he must be dead, therefore he can't marry anyone! If you put no and knew *why* you put no, then score another point.

Question 3, how many of each species? Who said two? . . . No. Who said one? . . . No. Who said it was Noah and not Moses who went into the Ark? Score one more point if you did.

Question 4, some months have 31 days, some months 30; how many have 28? Of course the answer is all of them, all 12 months have 28 days.

Question 5, Guy Fawkes and all that; do they have a 5th of November in America? Who put no? Well, I think the answer is yes; they do have a 5th of November, and a 6th of November, and a 7th of November. Score one more point for that.

Finally, *question 6,* and if you didn't get this we're really going to have some trouble; the plane flying over France and Germany; who said France? . . . No. Who said Germany? . . . No. Who said, 'they don't bury *survivors*?'

OK, tot up the marks out of six. How did you get on? Over many, many years of using that short listening test, the average mark has been two!

Right, here's another test. One to six down the side of the page. Are you ready?

I'm sorry to say I was pulling your leg, there isn't another test, but I would like you to try to analyse the feeling you have now, the feeling that you are really switched on to paying attention, that you are wired for sound. Do you feel different? I am sure that you do.

The skill of active listening is probably the greatest skill we need to have in selling. It is the skill that is least talked about but it is the one that will enable us to have the greatest success in what we do.

If we listen to our customers instead of talking to them all the time they will tell us what they want, tell us what they want to buy and they will usually tell us how to sell them our products, services or ideas. The same applies in all the areas of our lives: people will indicate how we can deal with them in all sorts of situations if we ask skilful questions and *actively* listen to the answers.

I often use analogies about golf. Do you play golf? Then try to think of listening in this way: the only time you never play a bad shot in golf is when the clubs are . . . still in the bag.

The only time we do not make mistakes in our jobs in selling is when we're not talking. We have two ears and one mouth and must try to use them in that proportion. Lee Iacocca, the boss of Chrysler in America, once said: 'The difference between a great company and a mediocre company is its ability to listen to its customers.'

We need that skill, the ability to listen actively to our customers. Some years ago, when I was the chairman of Compass Leasing plc, we were a leasing brokerage and we bought and sold money and arranged leasing contracts for our clients. I attended a meeting with one of our major finance-house funders in order to negotiate the price of the money we bought. I made my proposition and then asked for the order. The director of the finance company said, 'Peter, I don't think we can do that.' I said nothing but simply sat listening actively to the silence. After a moment or two of this pressuring silence the director turned round to me and said, 'Well, perhaps there is a way.' I replied with, 'How would it work?' After some moments' thought he went on to tell me. That reasonably short conversation made our business over £12,000 per month, nearly £150,000 per year and when the company was sold for a multiplication of profits, that conversation had made the shareholders over £900,000.

It's certainly true that good listeners are popular everywhere and studies show that it's good listeners who get the promotions, not necessarily the good talkers.

I am sure you can recall a situation where you have been out for a night with your friends and somebody starts to tell a joke; usually the subject of the joke prompts in your mind another joke. While the first joke is being told, instead of actively listening we are simply waiting for our turn to speak. That is the reason why during the next day we are unable to repeat the other jokes we heard in the evening: we were just waiting to speak.

I'm certain that in our profession as sales people we have the situation where our customers seem to say the same things in response to some of our questions, and I know that we've all been guilty of simply waiting to speak instead of actively listening to what the customer was saying.

So what are the steps to increase our ability in what I believe to be the key skill in selling?

The steps to success

Step 1

Listen 50 per cent of the time. Do you play chess? In that case you will know what a chess clock looks like. It's two clocks joined together with two switches. If I press the switch on my side it starts your clock, if you press the switch on your side it starts my clock. What would it be like if we were able to take a chess clock into all our sales conversations and recorded the amount of time we spoke and the amount of time the customer spoke? Would we be surprised to find out that we do most of the talking, instead of most of the listening? And yet it's only when the customer is talking that he or she is able to say that most important word . . . *Yes.* So let's listen for 50 per cent of the time.

Step 2

Listen for ideas as well as facts. If the customer comes up with a cold fact there is usually some reason for that statement. By skilful questioning and active listening we can find out the thoughts behind the fact; this may give us more information than the fact itself.

Step 3

Don't jump to conclusions, don't anticipate what the other person might say. We've all been in the situation, if we've been in selling for any time, where customers do say similar things and it's very easy for us to switch off our ears and jump to the conclusion that the customer is going to say exactly what somebody else said in response to the same question. It may *not* be the case and we could miss a vital opportunity to gather information. This gathering of information must be one of the first things we do when we're engaging in a sales conversation. How can we sell somebody something unless we've found out their needs and desires?

Step 4

Respond with 'Yes', 'Uh', 'Um', 'I see', to let the other person know you are *actively listening.* Have you ever been on a telephone call when suddenly the person on the other end of the line has said to you: 'Hello . . . hello . . . are you still there?' You know what's happened. You weren't responding to let the other person know you were listening. So in telephone calls and in face-to-face conversations, let the customers know you are listening to what they are saying.

Step 5

Make notes. I always believe that writing things down doesn't waste time, it simply uses time effectively. Making notes while a customer is talking can provide a first-rate base for our customer records. Customers will be pleasantly surprised if you are able to repeat back to them during this or subsequent meetings information they have passed on to you. In some situations it's courteous to ask if you may take notes.

Step 6

Don't judge *how* things are said. Even in a small country such as the United Kingdom there is a great variety of regional accents and if we get tied up with listening to *how* things are said we will often miss *what* is being said.

Some people speak very quickly, some people speak very slowly. Use your active listening skills to hear behind the speed of speech into the content and the ideas.

Step 7

Ask questions to clarify what is being said. Again, I am sure we've all been in a situation where we have said 'Yes' to indicate that we understood what another person was saying when in reality we didn't understand at all. Isn't it always the case that that 'Yes' will be caught out later. I have always found that customers are delighted to explain in greater detail the information they provide and if you are unsure of what is being said or the meaning of it simply ask. Don't say 'Yes' if you mean 'No'.

Step 8

Keep eye contact. That's not to say that you stare at your customer as though you were transfixed in the headlight beam of an oncoming car, but you actually do look in the customer's eyes so that they know you are listening. If you have difficulty looking in people's eyes directly, simply look at their foreheads. From anything but a short distance no one will be able to tell the difference.

Step 9

Watch body language, both yours and theirs. We are going to cover body language later so I will leave further thoughts until then.

Step 10

Don't finish other people's sentences. You might just get it wrong. We in selling tend to be quick minded and occasionally will come across a customer who speaks laboriously. You just have to wait.

Step 11

Pause before replying; it shows that you were listening and that you are giving a considered answer.

So what are the benefits of active listening? Well, I believe we become more likeable if we listen actively; I believe we have more success, that we have happier customers and contacts and that it really is the easiest way to sell our products, services or ideas.

What you need to do now is to prepare your action plan. An action plan on active listening is somewhat difficult. May I suggest you prepare a self-assessment test that you can use after, say, each of the next 21 sales calls? This will enable you to check if you have been actively listening.

On that active listening test you might put down such questions to yourself as those in the table opposite.

Memory

Tony Buzan states that the five keys to memory are primacy, immediacy, linking, unusual items and review.

Primacy means we tend to remember things at the start of any conversation or situation. Immediacy means that we tend to remember things at the end of a conversation or situation.

We also remember things or items of information that we are able to

Questions	1	2	3	4	5	6	7	8	9	10	11	12	13	14	15	16	17	18	19	20	21
1. Did I listen actively?																					
2. Did I listen for 50 per cent of the time?																					
3. Did I listen for ideas as well as facts?																					
4. Did I avoid jumping to conclusions?																					
5. Did I respond actively?																					
6. Did I make notes?																					
7. Did I avoid judging how things were said?																					
8. Did I ask questions to clarify information?																					
9. Did I maintain eye contact?																					
10. Did I avoid finishing others' sentences?																					

link to our previous experiences. If I turned up at your office in a pink suit with green spots you would be able to remember me until your dying days.

The final key to memory is review, which is why there is a review sheet at the end of this chapter. You may copy it, and the action plan, for all the other topics in this book.

Notes

Topic

Action plan

Name ______________________________

Topic ______________________ **Date** __________

Action	Target date	Completion date
1.		
2.		
3.		
4.		
5.		
6.		

Review plan

Name ______________________________

Topic ______________________ **Date** __________

Notes ______________________________

Action	Target date	Completion date
1.		
2.		
3.		
4.		
5.		
6.		

CHAPTER 2

Positive attitude

As always we are going to start with a quiz and on page 26 you will find the positive attitude test. Simply mark yourself out of 10 for your feelings about yourself, put the mark in the space provided between the two statements on each line. For example, if you really like yourself score 10; if you don't like yourself; score 1. Then add up the marks so that you have a positive attitude score out of 100.

Let's look at this subject of positive attitude and how it can impact on the jobs we do in selling.

In India, when they capture a baby elephant they chain the elephant by its hind leg to a wooden stake that has been driven into the ground. I'm sure you've seen that on films – it's a sort of telegraph pole that's been smashed on the top. Naturally, the baby elephant tries to break the chain and gain its freedom, but after a few days of pulling and falling down and hurting its leg it finally gives up. It realises that it cannot break the chain. It now believes it cannot break the chain ever and, as the elephant grows, the chain is *not,* repeat *not,* increased in size because the elephant still believes it cannot break it. Its self-belief, its attitude is that it cannot break that chain.

I have even heard that there have been instances where elephants have died in circus fires when they could have escaped and saved themselves, but they believed they could not break their chains. This seems hard to accept and yet I'm sure for all of us there are chains on our legs, chains on our attitude, chains on our minds that we've carried throughout our lives, some of them from our childhood.

The expression 'money is the root of all evil' is commonly used. The original quotation is 'the love of money is the root of all evil'. Money in itself is not evil, only the way in which it can be used. But of course it can be used for good.

One of my four sons is called Stephen and when he was only three he had to go into hospital for a small but somewhat painful operation. Naturally he had an injection to make him sleep through the operation. When he awoke, with a certain part of his anatomy in some pain, he made the obvious connection between the needle and the pain. Thereafter the word needle was immediately associated by him

Positive attitude

Write in your score between 10 and 1 for each pair of statements. 'I like myself': score 10 points. 'I don't like myself': score 1 point. Or somewhere in between.

I like myself		I don't like myself
I'm a winner		I'm a loser
I believe I can always learn something new		I believe there is not much more to learn
I'm happy		I'm unhappy
I'm enthusiastic		I'm unenthusiastic
I take 100 per cent responsibility for my actions		I sometimes blame others
I use positive self-talk		I use negative self-talk
I do the difficult things first		I leave the difficult things until last
I'm just the right age		I'm too young/old
I look on rejection as a learning opportunity		I fear rejection

Total score ☐

with pain (later in the book I'll be discussing neuro-linguistic programming and the anchoring effect of various incidents in our lives). The way we have changed that association for Stephen is simply to call things 'pins' instead of 'needles'; that doesn't create a problem for him.

Could it be that you could find by examination and self-questioning some of the chains you have been carrying around and take action to break them? You see, success is 90 per cent attitude, 10 per cent hard work and 10 per cent skill. What's wrong with that?

Yes, the mathematicians among you have worked out that that's 110 per cent, but that is often what it will take to be successful. A most important part in our make-up of success is attitude.

I heard a story years ago about a shoe company that wanted to expand. The management decided to send their best salesman to Africa. They sent him out there first class, booked him into a first-class hotel and when he arrived at the airport he went outside and then rushed straight back in. He phoned his boss and said: 'I'm coming straight home, it's a waste of time here, nobody wears shoes.'

The company decided to put off trying to sell in Africa. However, a couple of years later the company's management had changed and the idea came up again to expand into Africa. This time the most inexperienced salesman was sent, the new kid on the block. He was flown out 'tourist', booked into a cheap hotel and when he arrived at the airport he went outside and just like the other salesman rushed back into the airport and phoned his boss: 'Boss. Send three containers of shoes, it's great here, we'll make a fortune . . . nobody wears shoes.'

The only difference between the two salesmen was their 'attitude' to the situation. Are we looking at the opportunities or are we looking at the problems?

I once read that if we thought of opportunity and problem being at either end of a straight line, when we were looking at one we couldn't see the other. When we were looking at the problems we couldn't see the opportunities. When we were looking at the opportunities we were unable to see the problems.

I'm sure that, like me, over the years you've been down that road of selling and seen that massive company and decided that perhaps they were too big for you to call into their reception. Similarly, you have seen that small company and decided that they were too little to bother with; but, of course, that leads us into the situation of saying: 'I never go into companies with a green door, as I've never sold in a company with a green door before.' Our attitude can really make the difference to our success.

Just look at this number for a moment:

1 2 4 5 7 9

The question is, what's missing? In fact, there's nothing missing. I know I asked you what's missing in order to focus your minds on this particular question, but that's all too often what we do to ourselves. We look at what's missing and not at what's there. Who would like a bigger nose? Who would like less hair? Who would like to be fatter or slimmer?

It's strange, isn't it, that the women with straight hair want curly hair and the women with curly hair want straight hair, and fortunes are made by those companies dealing in the appropriate products to provide for that need.

Here is a suggestion: tonight when you go home, on your own, stand naked in front of a full-length mirror and fall in love with yourself again. There are certain parts you are not going to be able to change. Accept them! If there are things you can change then decide on the actions you need to take, set a goal and set about changing what you can. The rest accept; this year's model has already arrived.

Have any of you ever been drunk in your life? Go on, admit it. Imagine this situation. You got up one morning and walked, somewhat the worse for wear, towards the top of the stairs. At the top of the stairs you tripped and fell down the stairs and broke your leg. Having been taken to the hospital, having had the leg reset and put in plaster, you're lying in your bed feeling somewhat stupid. Your friends and family come to see you and most of them ask the question:

'Does it hurt?'

'It sure does hurt, I feel so stupid.'

Imagine a different situation: it's Friday lunchtime, you've gone to the bank to cash a cheque so that you have some money for the weekend. While you are in the bank two gunmen burst in to hold up the bank and steal the money. In a fit of bravery you tackle the gunmen, save the money, save the bank, save the people and, in due time, appear in the local papers with tributes to your bravery. Unfortunately, during your heroic act you break your leg, you're taken off to hospital, the leg is reset and put in plaster and there you are lying at home in your bed. People come to see you, family and friends, and they ask the obvious question:

'Does it hurt?'

'No . . . it's nothing!'

What those stories clearly tell us is that it is our attitude that changes reality.

To be successful in our jobs we only have to be a little bit better at a 1,000 things not a 1,000 times better at one thing. The racehorse that wins the race doesn't usually do so by many lengths, it's often just a short head – yet the winnings of the winning horse are often five or even ten times those of the horses that do not win.

Let us decide now to improve in all the areas of our selling career just by 1 per cent; just think what the compounding effect of all that would be.

The first step in being successful in anything we do is deciding to be successful, getting our attitude right, deciding to be successful and deciding to pay the price of success or perhaps more importantly the price of failure.

Picture the situation: you're lying in bed, it's a cold and frosty morning, your heating has broken down or there is a sudden cold snap and you hadn't put the heating on. The bed is warm and yet the room is freezing. Physically getting out of bed is usually a simple process; one leg and then the other leg, stand up and away you go, but actually *deciding* to get out of bed, that's the hard part.

I have this idea called the Maradonna Principle. If you are on the pitch in the middle of the game and wanting to score, from time to time you are going to be kicked, you're going to be tripped and you're going to be fouled. That's the price of trying to score. But if you are on the touchline as a linesman you won't get kicked, you won't get tripped and you won't get fouled, but neither will you score. I believe we should welcome the fouls. It shows us we are on our way to success.

Studies show that success, and particularly success in sales, is not determined by age or sex or education or creed or colour or weight or height. It is determined by attitude. I once saw in a monthly magazine called *Bits and Pieces* a list of school reports of famous people. It was said that:

- George Bernard Shaw was a bad speller.
- Benjamin Franklyn was poor in maths.
- Salvador Dali and Edgar Allan Poe were expelled.
- Thomas Edison was bottom of the class.
- Einstein was considered mentally slow.
- Lincoln and Henry Ford showed no promise.

It just goes to show that sometimes people don't recognise our true talents. If we have the attitude that we *can* succeed, then we have taken the first step to success.

Success is made by mental attitude, not by mental capacities. *Poor is a state of mind, broke is a state of pocket.*

So let's move on to the steps, steps to having a more positive mental attitude in all the areas of our lives.

The steps to success

Step 1

'Decide on the price of success' and decide to pay that price. Although that's an oft-used expression in sales, perhaps it would be more important to decide on the price of failure. Wouldn't it be a terrible situation to arrive at a point in your life and look back over your life and say: 'If only I'd . . . I wouldn't be a failure today' ? Surely that is the heaviest price we can ever pay, so decide on that price.

Step 2

Be enthusiastic. By that I don't mean so hyper-enthusiastic that you will frighten people away. But be enthusiastic about your company, about your product or services and about yourself. Sometimes we just have to 'Fake it, until we make it.' Let's start to be enthusiastic; if we only pretend to be enthusiastic it's amazing how genuinely enthusiastic we become.

I remember a situation when I worked for an American company called Diversey which had about 300 salespeople in the United Kingdom. I worked on their catering division. Our Midland sales-team meetings were held in a back room at Keele Service Station on the M6 motorway and at one such meeting our area manager, Lou Franks, from Coventry came along. He was there to tell us about a new product that Diversey were launching. He was so enthusiastic about it; he was smiling and happy and couldn't wait to tell us about this new product which was . . . an oven cleaner. Can you imagine getting excited about an oven cleaner?

Anyway, he was and he told us all about it. He had been down to Cockfosters, the head office of Diversey, and there had seen a demonstration of this new green gunge. If you spread it on the door of an oven, a commercial oven that had not been cleaned for perhaps five or ten years, and left the green gunge for some ten minutes, when you wiped it away the oven would sparkle and again look like new.

He was so enthusiastic about this product that during the next month we sold more oven cleaner than in the months to come. This wasn't because the product didn't work, it did! As usual with Diversey, it was an excellent product and lived up to its claims, but we simply sold it on enthusiasm.

Step 3

When you have negative thoughts, say out loud . . . 'Cancel'. The whole idea of this is to have a key word or a habit breaker that switches us out of negative mode into positive mode. It needn't be my word 'Cancel'. You can think of any word that will snap you back into a positive state.

We all get negative thoughts from time to time and might say such things as:

'Perhaps I'm too old to do this?'

'I don't feel up to it today.'

And so on. We just need a way to snap back into our positive, can-do attitude.

Step 4

If you're feeling low, switch into manager mode, manager of yourself. The way I look at sales and commercial life in general is that we all work for Me Limited, or perhaps better, Me *un*limited, and some of us simply hire out our services to one particular company. If we take responsibility for ourselves then we don't really need a manager; perhaps what we may be looking for is a leader. That seems a hard-line statement. Let me explain it in the following way.

Imagine you were the manager of . . . you. Then you would know all the facets of your personality, what makes you get up in the morning, what keeps you going in the hard times during the day, and wouldn't it therefore be easy to manage someone like that? But of course you can; by switching into 'manager mode' and having conversations with yourself, you can find your own answers.

I always use the mirror for that self-management idea and in the various companies I ran had mirrors on the sales desk. By simply looking clearly into your own eyes and asking the sorts of question that a manager might ask you, you know when you're telling the truth. You can find all the honest answers to such questions as:

- How many sales calls are you going to do today?
- Why is it that your figures aren't as good this month?
- How am I going to sell more during the next year?

You already know the answers.

Step 5

Practise being positive. Success depends on your opinion of you and, after all, life is a mirror: if you smile at the world it smiles back; if you frown at the world it frowns back; if you're honest with the world it will be honest back to you.

Step 6

Say, 'I like myself'. Some years ago on an audio-tape programme from America I heard this idea from the excellent speaker Brian Tracy of saying to yourself 'I like myself'.

When I first heard it I thought it was a bit over the top, but having tried it I realised how powerful it was. I used it for myself, I shared the idea with the members of my salesforce and we had such fun with it that we use it on a regular basis and even at company meetings with over 60 people chanting together, 'I like myself.'

The idea, while simple, can provide an electric atmosphere if you're on your own or in a group and if you use it as you're going along the road towards the next sales call. It's amazing what positive feelings you have when you get out of the car. It's almost as if, when someone shakes hands with you, they get an electric shock.

Step 7

Be honest with yourself and your customers. If you honestly have the benefit of your product or service for the customer clearly in your mind and that is your prime motivation, then that will shine out of your eyes and customers will know you're being honest. After all, *our success is simply a by-product of our customers' success.*

Step 8

Decide to undergo life-long learning. If you examine any salesforce and look at the person in that force who has the best pure sales ability but is missing in other areas then that person will *not* be the top sales person.

Similarly, if you look at the person with the top product knowledge, they probably won't be the top performer either. But if you look at the person with good sales skills and good product knowledge who has their personal development in high gear, invariably they are the top performer.

By personal development I mean attitude, personality, setting goals, charisma, drive, enthusiasm, confidence, personal power, self-belief, the ability to handle rejection and, most importantly, maintaining a positive attitude towards learning new skills. I once saw it written as 'minds are like parachutes, they only work when they are open.'

Let us listen to new tapes and read books; let's stop using our car radios as chewing-gum for the ears and turn our cars into colleges on wheels.

Our success potential is calculated by selling skills *plus* product knowledge *multiplied* by personal development training. Rate yourself now on those three areas and see what your success potential could be.

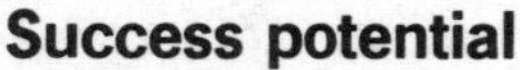

Success potential

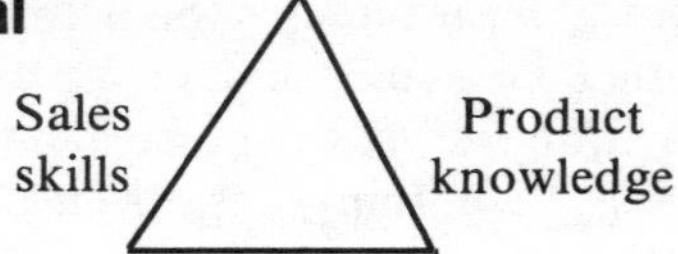

Sales skills	+	Product knowledge	×	Personal development training	=	Success potential

Decide on a mark out of 10 for your level in each of the three areas. Then calculate your success potential.

Before reading this book

☐ + ☐ × ☐ = ☐

After reading this book

☐ + ☐ × ☐ = ☐

Step 9

Take 100 per cent responsibility for your life and your actions.

If our attitude is that there is always someone else to blame, I believe that will hold us back from success. If we determine that we are the prime factor in our success, our chances have greatly improved.

Step 10

Surround yourself with positive people. It's back to the old expression about the bad apple in the barrel, isn't it? If you have one negative person in the salesforce that person can damage all the others.

If you are a sales manager and you have a negative person on your staff, it is your duty to make them positive or get rid of them. While this may seem a hard-line attitude, I firmly believe that a sales team or even a whole company can be crippled by the attitude of one person.

I remember once going to an Institute of Bankers' dinner in the West Midlands and one of the after-dinner speakers was a well-known local estate agent called Mark Kenchington. Part of his speech was the story about his father and his school teacher.

His father had always been totally supportive, totally positive with him, telling Mark that he could achieve anything he wanted. The school teacher Miss Gibbons, on the other hand, had always had the opposite view, saying such things as: 'Kenchington, you'll never amount to anything.'

He continued his story by saying: 'Well, here I am, standing in front of 1200 people at the Institute of Bankers' dinner as the after-dinner speaker and I would just like to say a few words.'

He looked towards the ceiling and said: 'My father and Miss Gibbons have unfortunately passed on so I'd like to say:

Dad, thank you for all your support.

Miss Gibbons, # ~ * !'

His comments brought the house down and the point of the story was obvious; we all need to surround ourselves with positive people, positive people who believe in our ability to succeed.

This positiveness also applies to the newspapers and TV. We really don't need all the horrific details of the happenings in today's troubled world: the simple headlines are often sufficient for our knowledge and use in our selling career.

Let me share with you some excellent positive attitude expressions I picked up over the years:

- It's not what you know: it's what you *do* with what you know, that counts.
- Success comes in cans, not cannots.
- Success comes after you've paid the price, never before.
- If you do what you always did, you'll get what you always got.
- The definition of a miracle is doing today exactly what you did yesterday and expecting a different result.
- You're never on holiday from yourself.

CHAPTER 3

Avoiding procrastination

Let us now move on to avoiding procrastination. Procrastination can be defined as 'putting off until tomorrow the things we know we really should do today'; and, as always, we start with a test. As you will see, there are simply three questions to answer.

Question 1

Give five reasons why people procrastinate.

1. ______________________________

2. ______________________________

3. ______________________________

4. ______________________________

5. ______________________________

Question 2

Give three results of procrastination.

1. ______________________________

2. ______________________________

3. ______________________________

Question 3

Give three results of avoiding procrastination.

1. ______________________________

2. ______________________________

3. ______________________________

Let's consider the reasons why people procrastinate:

1. To escape the task in the hope that it will go away.
2. Fear of failure.

3. Poor time management.
4. Haven't set goals.
5. Hope that somebody else will do the task.
6. Don't have enough information to complete the task.
7. They are in the wrong job.
8. They don't like doing the task.
9. They focus on the whole task instead of bits of it.
10. Haven't got priorities in order.

I am sure we could come up with another 20 or even 30 reasons why people procrastinate.

What about the second question, what are the downside results of procrastinating? A lowering of self-esteem and self-confidence. We have a negative attitude and begin to doubt our own ability to perform; we get frustrated and we become known as a 'can't do' person.

Now for the third question; if we're able to avoid procrastination we get more things done, we have a greater sense of achievement and therefore our self-confidence and self-esteem go up: we become known as a 'can do' person.

So how are we going to beat procrastinating? How are we really going to get more and more things achieved in our lives? How are we going to take more steps on the road to success?

Well, it's always stated that the longest journey starts with one step, so very often it really is a case of just doing the first thing. We've mentioned before that deciding is the difficult part and doing the easy part.

I've seen it put in a couple of different ways. One was called 'How to eat an elephant,' the answer simply being one bite at a time. And the other was on an audio-tape that discussed the Salami Principle and that's the one I always think of. The idea is as follows: imagine you have gone into the local delicatessen and there hanging above the counter is a large salami. It is 18 inches long and 4 inches thick and it's covered with bits of string and odd bits of fat and grease. I'm sure that most of us, even if we liked salami, could not bring ourselves to eat it all in one go. However, if we asked the grocer to put it on the machine and slice it into thin slices then, provided we liked salami, I am sure we could eat all of it.

This is exactly the same with most of the tasks we tackle; so often we are looking at the whole task, *all* the things we need to accomplish, when really what we need to do is to break it down into thin slices, into bite-size chunks and then simply tackle them one at a time. So let's look at the steps for avoiding procrastination.

The steps to success

Step 1

Just decide to get started and then get started. I always use the Three Ds Principle, which stands for Do it, Delegate it or Dump it. If you don't do it and don't delegate it you might as well dump it because it's not going to get done. You can use the Three Ds Principle for all sorts of areas.

Step 2

Plot it out. The way I do this is to take my A4 pad and write a question at the top of the page focusing on the end result; for example, 'What do I need to do in order to . . . ?' Then I simply write down, as fast as I possibly can, all the actions I know I will need to take to achieve the desired result.

Next, having broken it down into bite-sized pieces, I prioritise that list or put it into order; however, I always do it twice, and I suggest you do too. It's what the old carpet fitters used to say: 'Measure it twice and cut it once.'

Who at the moment has a task they have been putting off, they've been procrastinating about? You've got to decorate the lounge? OK, let's work through the steps on paper.

Calculate cost, decide on colour, buy materials, clear the room, prepare the surfaces, paint the woodwork, hang the paper, celebrate.

decide on colour	calculate cost
buy materials	decide on colour
calculate cost	buy materials
prepare the surfaces	clear the room
clear the room	prepare the surfaces
hang the paper	paint the woodwork
paint the woodwork	hang the paper
celebrate	celebrate

We can see from this simple example how useful it is to measure it twice and cut it once because our second list clearly shows a different order of priority from our first list. Use that idea – it works well.

Step 3

Do the first step now, calculate the cost.

Step 4

Again, make sure you can do it. Having decided you are going to do it and not delegate it or dump it, having worked out the actions you need to take – the salami slices – and having decided the order in which those actions need to be taken, before we really launch it let's just make sure we can physically or mentally complete the task.

Years ago I used to collect Vesta boxes – the early types of silver matchboxes. I had quite a reasonable collection, which I wanted to display. I attended a local antique market held on a Sunday at a local hotel and bought (at an extremely low cost) a glass-topped display cabinet. I took it home and, having the materials to hand, decided first to sand down the cabinet with rough paper and then with smooth paper so I could subsequently varnish it and re-glaze it. In my enthusiasm I started with the rough sandpaper. Having got halfway through the job I rushed the balance; I really wanted to get on with the fine sandpaper and the varnishing, which I did with disastrous results. Bits of sandpaper everywhere, dust in the brush and a totally unprofessional job. I put it to one side, determined to re-do it on another occasion. You might guess what happened: I simply didn't get round to it, I procrastinated. I then looked through my notes on procrastination and realised when I reached step 4 that this was not a job for me. I telephoned an old friend who was into woodwork and he agreed to do it for me just as a favour. Today I still have that cabinet, re-glazed, re-varnished and in excellent order.

The purpose of the story? Make absolutely certain you can do it before you get into the task so that you can (in the words of the one-minute manager) 'catch yourself doing it right'.

Step 5

If you're having difficulty with procrastination use this idea. List as many successes as you can that you've had over your life; this may be attending a particular school, passing certain exams, getting a certain job, passing your driving test or a variety of others. When you look back over a list of successes it reminds you of what you can do and persuades you to get on and do.

Step 6

If you normally have difficulty completing tasks, begin each day with the most unpleasant task and then everything else seems simple.

For example, go to that sock or underwear drawer and tip all the contents in the middle of the bedroom floor. Sort them out, throw away the unwearable ones, put all the colours back together in the proper order and put the drawer back. What a fantastic feeling this will set up in your mind for the start of any day.

It has always been said that the reason people don't buy the new clothes they want is that there is no space in the wardrobe to put them. Perhaps what we could do is go to that wardrobe, ignore the little voice that comes from the back that says, 'You'll need me again one day,' sort out those clothes, give them away to charity or throw away those that will never fit again or those you will never wear again and create that space. You will find you are then motivated to buy new clothes and motivated to have sufficient success to generate the money to buy those clothes.

With sales calls or problems, do the difficult calls first, then the rest are easy. Is there a call, perhaps a telephone call, you've been putting off?

Here's a tip. Finishing the job is not completion. To achieve completion, get someone else to look at the job and congratulate you on having achieved it.

You know the situation: you've cleared out your garage one Sunday morning, you've taken out all those jars with paint brushes stuck to the bottom that are never going to be used again. You've thrown away all those rusty nails you've hoarded for years that will never be used, and you've finally decided that tin of paint in that unusual colour will never get its airing again. When the task is completed call your partner, proudly show them the garage and invariably they will respond with, 'Well done! It looks great.'

Step 7

Whatever action you've decided to take, just try to do it for about 15 minutes. You can usually do anything for 15 minutes – it just gets you started. You'll be amazed how 15 minutes will turn into 30 and 45 and 60 minutes and, before you know where you are, you're halfway towards the task being completed. Just get started.

Step 8

Tell the world. With goal setting, it's *not* a good idea – repeat, *not* a good idea – to share your goals, but more of that later. However, to avoid procrastination on most minor items, committing publicly will create pressure for you to accomplish the task.

Step 9

Decide on a reward for yourself when the task is complete.

Step 10

Become a computer and just do it. Imagine you have created with your prioritisation a computer program, which you simply had to plug into a mechanical being who would then proceed to execute all the tasks in order. Could you be that robot? I am sure you could.

Let me therefore summarise avoiding procrastination as: *decide, plan, slice* and *do.*

At a seminar, I took a £20 note out of my pocket and slipped it under the corner of the board, in full view of everyone, and said, 'Who would like this £20 note?' Of course, everyone nodded and said 'yes'.

I followed that with, 'How do you get it?'

A variety of suggestions were thrown up; from an exchange for another £20 note, to bribery, to physical force, to selling a product and numerous others.

I simply kept on nodding and saying 'yes' until finally Fiona, a very positive girl, jumped up, ran to the front and took the £20 note from the corner of the flip chart and ran back to her seat.

'It's yours!' I said. 'Please keep it. There are only prizes in this life for taking action. All the good ideas are of no use at all until somebody does something with them. Hopefully, this little demonstration will remind us all in the future that taking action really is the key, and no doubt Fiona will buy us all a drink in the bar at lunchtime.'

CHAPTER 4

Why people buy

Let's start with a quiz. Write down ten reasons why you believe people buy your particular product or service.

1. ______________________________
2. ______________________________
3. ______________________________
4. ______________________________
5. ______________________________
6. ______________________________
7. ______________________________
8. ______________________________
9. ______________________________
10. ______________________________

I think we can summarise all these into four major categories, which are gain, pain, crowd and proud. The first two are the most important. All of us do things for two major reasons: to gain or get pleasure or to avoid pain. Of course, crowd and proud fit nicely into those two as well. We want the pleasure of being part of the crowd and therefore avoiding the pain of loneliness; or we want to be proud of our acquisition and have the pleasure of that pride.

I will discuss at some length later the features and benefits of purchasing, but first let's remember that people don't buy matches – they buy flames; people don't buy drill bits – they buy holes. All the research says that people buy emotionally and not logically. If someone tells you they are buying logically it's simply that they experience more emotion in that particular piece of logic. We're all trying to gain the benefits or to avoid the pain, and the stronger emotion always wins.

If you feel someone is buying to be part of the crowd – and some buyers like to own something others have tried and tested – you will need to have testimonial letters, and that is covered in greater detail in the section on closing, Chapter 10.

All customers have three choices when it comes to buying: they can decide to buy from you, they can buy from another company selling a similar product or they can buy from no one at all. The easiest way to find out the answers to those three implied questions is simply to ask.

My suggestion is that you go to four different people and ask them why they buy. Those four could be:

1. Your boss
2. The buyer of your company
3. A customer
4. Yourself.

You may go pre-armed with the following list and ask each of those four people to put these factors in order regarding a buying decision:

1. The product or service itself
2. Variations on the product
3. Delivery terms
4. The salesperson
5. The price
6. The terms
7. The accuracy of information or the product
8. The supplying company's reputation
9. The venue or setting
10. Breakdowns and problems.

If you find the people you ask are extremely helpful about this, ask them to put the list into order for *three* different products to see if there are variations purely by product alone.

The next question we must surely ask ourselves is, could it be that customers buy in the same way as we buy?

If the ten factors above are not relevant to your particular product or service, change them to make them relevant, and take them along to show those three people, the boss, the buyer and your customers.

Could it be that one of the major factors in the success or failure of any sale is the salesperson concerned? If so, what are the important features? The following 20 are some of my ideas:

1. Appearance
2. The salesperson listened to the customer
3. The salesperson was looking for a long-term relationship
4. The salesperson's ability to close the sale helped the buyer to buy

5. The smile and attitude of the salesperson
6. The salesperson was honest
7. The experience of the salesperson
8. The salesperson's ability to handle questions
9. The salesperson's ability to come up with creative solutions
10. The salesperson's positive attitude
11. The fact that benefits and not just features were discussed
12. An agenda had been prepared that was well thought-out; planned questions were asked
13. The call itself had been planned
14. The salesperson was confident in him or herself and in the company
15. If the salesperson was a woman she didn't flirt or if the salesperson was a man he didn't flirt with the buyer or office staff to get the order
16. The type of handshake given
17. The salesperson was punctual
18. The salesperson did not criticise competitors or his or her own head-office staff
19. The opening statement made by the salesperson set the scene for the whole conversation
20. The salesperson had a meaningful reason for attending a second meeting.

Let us take a few moments now to look at that list and decide if there are any areas in which *we* can improve. Simply tick them off and then add them to your action plan.

Next, I would like you to imagine the last three times you *didn't* buy a product that was being sold to you or that you wanted to buy. Answer this question: 'Why didn't you buy?' Write down the main reason for each of those occasions on page 44.

Now imagine the last three times you made a sale. Was the difference . . . you? I believe it probably was, because sometimes our sales activity prevents sales and sometimes it makes the sale. Write down the main reasons why you succeeded on the last three successful sales.

Next question: what about the last three times you didn't sell, when you failed to make a sale? Write down three main reasons why you failed.

My suggestion is that you go back to the 30-question self-assessment test (page 12) we did at the start to see if there are any factors in there that will prompt you to remember why you were unsuccessful on three occasions.

Three reasons why I didn't buy:

1. ______________________________

2. ______________________________

3. ______________________________

Three reasons why I did make a sale:

1. ______________________________

2. ______________________________

3. ______________________________

Three reasons why I didn't make a sale:

1. ______________________________

2. ______________________________

3. ______________________________

It is always a good idea to be self-analytical; however, that is not to say that we only look at the negatives. We need to look at the positives too. Of course, let's not get into the paralysis of analysis so that we are spending so much time analysing that we don't have time to do any sales calls. However, if we analyse each call afterwards to see why we made a sale or why we failed to make a sale, that self-learning can only assist us in plotting our path to success.

Could it be that some of the reasons customers don't buy is that they are worried about making a decision? Good testimonial letters will help you to overcome this point.

Some of our customers simply won't decide. They procrastinate or prevaricate. I try to overcome this by a method I call the Total Offer Concept, that is reiterating the major benefits relevant to that particular customer and then asking for the order again.

Some customers simply don't understand our product's concept or use, and in this situation we need to go slowly, carefully explaining the benefits and asking questions in order to make sure we are customising our conversation to the buyer's needs.

Some customers are understandably loyal to their current suppliers. This can be very good news for us because, if we are able to change the customer to buying the supplies from us, then we know there is a chance the customer will remain loyal.

The way we all handle this difficult area is to go slowly and ask the customer such questions as: '*If ever* you were to change, what would make you do it?' I have found that customers, in response to this question, will go off on a long, rambling dissertation and it may be necessary to ask the question again, stressing the 'if ever'. The real answer to this question will give you the customer's main desire or hot button and, if we are able honestly to supply our products or services based on the customer's needs, we have increased our chances of a successful sale.

Let's briefly summarise at this point. All customers buy emotionally, not logically. There are four areas of motivation: gain, pain, proud and crowd. If we undertake our analysis with ourselves, our bosses, the buyer in our own companies and our customers, we will soon compile a major list of reasons why people buy, particularly why they buy our product. We can then use this information to tailor our proposals to future prospects.

Name	**Type**	**How to deal**
Bert	Boss	Give concise information and close
Ian	Impulsive	Be enthusiastic
Steve	Stubborn	Repackage the information until a decision is reached
Henry	Henpecked	Make sure the other decision-makers are present
Susan	Sarcastic	Either ignore the sarcasm or leave
Stephanie	Silent	Ask lots of open questions
Tony	Talkative	When Tony takes a breath, jump in: it may be your only chance
Alan	Arguer	Respond with 'Yes, I can understand that your experience would indicate that point of view and . . .'
Charlie	Changeable	As each point is agreed, note it on paper with a large tick at the side
Adam	Aggressive	Keep your cool
Nigel	Know-it-all	Keep smiling and ask lots of questions
George	Go slowly	Again, use the idea of ticking the agreed points and go slowly to match his style

As Keith Floyd, the well-known TV chef, once remarked: 'Business is fun even though it's not funny.'

We need to tailor our approach and benefit statements so they are relevant to the buyer in question. Sales directors are concerned with turnover; managing directors tend to be concerned with profit; financial directors are more concerned with cost; and works directors with the actual operation of the business. They all have different hot buttons and it is only by asking well-thought-out, pre-planned questions that we will discover those hot buttons and be able to press them to create the results profitable to both parties.

If, when you are discussing your products with the customers, you carefully watch their body language you will see their eyes light up. You will see them leaning forward. You will see them become excited when you mention a point about which they are keen. Watch carefully, use the information you have gathered.

So what are the steps? What do we need to do to be skilful at understanding why people buy?

The steps to success

Step 1

Design for yourself a 'picture of a customer form'. This is a simple form that has, down the left-hand side, all the possible reasons why your customers buy your products. By skilful questioning and keeping careful records you will find the hot buttons for each customer. This information can be transferred to your customer record information so that you can review it before any sales call with any customer.

Step 2

Listen carefully. We have discussed active listening in some depth and I have always found that most customers will tell you what you need to say and do in order to complete a sale.

Step 3

Features and benefits: we need to concentrate on selling the benefits and results of our products and not simply the features.

Step 4

Appearance. In today's professional market-place we all need to be aware of our image. If we are well presented, if our cars, briefcases and samples are well presented, we are increasing our chances of success.

Step 5

Focus on the customer. All customers will be aware if you are focused on the amount of money you are to make from the sale. If we can honestly focus on the benefit for the customer this would clearly show in our eyes and speech and persuade people to buy. After all, people need to buy people before they buy products.

Step 6

Be a problem-solver. Most sales are based on the solving of a problem – namely, the avoidance of pain – and then turning the situation round so that we can focus on the pleasure for the customer in owning our product or using our service. After all, if there is no cavity there can be no filling.

Step 7

Balance the appeal of the sale between left and right brain. It is always said that the left brain is the logical side and the right brain the creative side (albeit that recent research says we are able to be creative with both sides of our brain). Make sure we are appealing to the emotional side and backing this up with clear financial information.

Step 8

Be enthusiastic – not over-enthusiastic, but enthusiastic to the point where customers will be aware that you are convinced of the value of your product, convinced of the ability of your company to provide the service required.

Step 9

Be patient. Customers do take time to make purchases. Some people will decide instantly on a purchase of several thousand pounds, others will take for ever over a £25 item. Be patient; allow them the thinking time necessary to make that decision.

Step 10

Be honest. Research says that upset customers tell nine other people and that happy customers tell only five people. If we are dishonest with our customers then we have started on the slippery slope to financial failure.

Let's move on to the action plan. First, it is an excellent idea to get testimonial letters from your clients so they can be used in the sales situation. A testimonial is simply a letter from a happy customer on company letterhead clearly stating how pleased the customer is with your product and how it's benefiting the customer and his or her company.

The second action I believe we need to take is the self-assessment test on why people buy, and to check ourselves after the next 30 calls to make sure we are being our most effective.

Action three: do the question list (page 42) for your boss, the buyer, the customer and yourself.

Action four, keep records.

We all have different entry-skill levels to all the topics discussed so far, and therefore all our action plans will be different. If you are having any difficulty whatsoever in completing and compiling the action plan, simply go back to the steps. If you agree with my thoughts on increasing our abilities, use the steps as the guide to your action plan.

My final thought on why people buy. I've found that customers often buy because they know the salesperson cares. The ways we can show we care are many:

1. Let's send thank-you notes for the orders we take.
2. Make sure we know the secretary's name and the receptionist's name.
3. Be knowledgeable about the client's business and the market in which the client operates.
4. Watch the papers and send congratulation notes if appropriate.
5. Really care.

CHAPTER 5

Open and closed questions

Let us now move on to our next topic, open and closed questions. Please answer in the space provided below the two questions: What is an open question? and What is a closed question?

What is an open question?

What is a closed question?

A variety of ideas on open and closed questions will be given, and I think we could look at them in this way. We use open questions to let the customer tell us the information we need so that we will be able to supply the right product. We use closed questions to bring customers back on line if they have been talking for too long or to solicit precise information in small amounts.

I think of it in this way: information is power and it is certainly true that, in today's technological and fast communications age, information really can provide power.

Throughout our sales or business careers most of us have been taught or have taken the time to learn many of the skills of giving out information. We give presentations about our products, our services or ideas, yet during those presentations the information only moves in one direction: towards the customer. If information is power, those presenting are simply giving power and not receiving it.

During our sales conversations we need to remain in control. We need to direct, lead and help the customers to buy our products or services.

Imagine you're fishing, you've baited your hook, cast out and the fish has taken the bait. The fish swims up and down the river but you are still in control – at any time you can strike and reel in: the decision is yours. That is the power of open and closed questions.

Open questions let the fish run. Closed questions bring it back. Rudyard Kipling gives us the main openers for the open questions we can ask:

'I keep six honest serving men,
They taught me all I knew,
Their names are *what* and *why* and *when*
And *how* and *where* and *who.*'

I am sure you have found that people prefer to talk rather than listen and, as successful sales people, we prefer to listen. So it suits both of us. Good questions make people like you, and if you ask enough questions people will talk to you all day. Answers will tell you how customers feel, how they think, how they see the situation you are describing, and questions can remove misunderstanding.

The ability to ask questions is the sign of a good salesperson; the ability to ask well-thought-out, structured questions is the sign of a great salesperson. If we use questions skilfully they will help us to qualify a prospective customer. They will uncover whether or not the customer is aware of our product or service; they will uncover the customer's authority or otherwise to buy, his or her ability to buy and the possible need or desire for our products.

Questions involve the buyer in a buying/selling problem-solving process and stop the situation being a one-way street with the salesperson simply presenting a pre-learned patter or spiel.

There is an excellent story about Charles Luckman, who was a salesman with Colgate Palmolive. On one of his first calls he called into a chemist shop and the *blunt* chemist, after Luckman had introduced himself, simply said:

'I don't want any soap.'

Luckman smiled and said:

'I know you don't. If you'd wanted any you'd have called. I came round to find out why you don't want any. Don't your customers buy soap?'

What an excellent question that was. That question and Luckman's ideas ensured he became President of Colgate Palmolive at the tender age of 37 years, having started as a salesman with the company.

Knowing that questions really do give us the power in any commercial situation, let's move forward and look at the steps to improve our ability in this art of asking careful, thought-out, well-structured questions.

The steps to success

Step 1

List 20 open-ended questions: you can use in a sales situation. For example: 'Tell me, Mr. Customer, how did you become involved in this business? What are your plans for the future of the company? How do you see the salesforce expanding over the next few years? What is your view regarding the export potential of your products?'

Step 2

List 20 closed questions you can use in a sales situation. For example: 'How many staff do you have? Do you like it in blue? Do you have any branches from which the company operates? Is it important when you take delivery? Is it important that the product has this special attachment?'

As you will realise, some of these closed questions are in themselves trial closing opportunities to find out the customer's potential need and the customer's agreement to the points you are making. I'll discuss closing in greater detail when we move into that particular topic (Chapter 10).

Step 3

Mark up your best 10 open-ended questions and your best 10 closed questions. You'll know which are best because they will be the ones that will solicit the maximum amount of information you need to customise your product to the client's desires and needs. Then you will need to practise those questions again and again and again until you can use them smoothly and effectively. After all, *Necessity is the mother of invention, but repetition is the master of skill.*

Step 4

Practise using this response: 'I don't know, what do you think?' or a variation of it. What this question does is prove that you are not a 'know-all' and it also enables you to see the situation from the customer's point of view.

Step 5

Practise this question so you may use it at the start of all your sales conversations: 'Who, apart from you, will be involved in making the final decision?' The purpose of this question is to establish that the customer has the money, the authority and the need – what has often been called the 'man'.

The implication of the question is that the customer does have the authority to make a decision but may need others' agreement if the amount of money involved is above the customer's personal limit.

Step 6

Decide to use questions as the main tool of your trade, not statements. Statements will give information, questions will *gather* information.

Step 7

Listen carefully to the answers. My suggestion is that you try to become like a successful and professional TV interviewer. Use silence after your open questions. If you watch the good interviewers, particularly the good chat-show hosts, you will find they ask an open question and after the guest has responded the interviewer will say . . . nothing at all. This will prompt the guest into expanding the answer. If we use this idea in our sales careers we can very gently, by using only the pressure of silence, persuade our customers to give us a greater depth of information regarding their use of our product or service.

Try to think of questions as the club in your golfer's or salesperson's bag. It is only by constant practice of our skills in this area that we can reach for that club, welcome it as an old friend and use it with accuracy and precision to achieve the result we desire.

CHAPTER 6

Communication skills

We are now going to discuss communication skills, which fall into four main areas. First *what* we say; second, *how* we say it; third, our *body language* and the customer's body language; and, fourth *how* to read the customers by watching their eyes.

As always we'll start with our usual test or quiz to focus our minds. Experts say that our three main areas of communication – namely, what, how and body language – each have a different percentage of importance. What do you think those percentages are?

What we say ______

How we say it ______

Body language ______

= 100 per cent

According to the information from the experts, and I must admit when I first heard these percentages I doubted the figures, what we say is 7 per cent important; how we say it 38 per cent; and body language is 55 per cent important in communication.

Now I know that seems heavily weighted in favour of body language but, having spent many years since I first read that information studying body language and developing my skills in that area, I have come to believe the experts.

Let's move on to this first part and discuss *what we say.*

What we say

The words we actually use should be determined to some degree by the person to whom we are speaking. If we are able to reflect the type of language used by our customers they will feel more at ease.

There are two ways in which we can build rapport with others.

1. Reflect back the words they use. We might use industry jargon if the customer uses it, or we can repeat the words the customer uses.
2. Use the ideas from neuro-linguistic programming (NLP). In the

early 1970s, Bandler and Grinder discovered that we all have a 'home base' of language, namely visual, auditory or kinesthetic (there is more about this in Chapter 20). By using words from the customer's home base we can build rapport at a subconcious level.

While on first examination these ideas seem somewhat strange, I can confirm that more and more people understand the principles of NLP and are using them, not only in the area of building rapport but also in creating personal change. In Chapter 20 we discuss NLP and its strengths in creating change, but for now we will concentrate on three main types of people and the language they use.

1. Visual

Visually based people use all the words we would associate with seeing. For example, they will say such things as 'it *appears* to me', 'that's a short-*sighted* point of view', 'I'm *eye to eye* with you on that', 'it *looks* to me like', 'I get the *picture*' – and all those types of expression that clearly say that their thinking process is, *at that moment,* in a visual mode.

When you meet a visual person, that is to say somebody who uses all these sight images, they may well say, 'nice to *see* you' and when they leave they may say, 'I look forward to *seeing* you again.'

Visual people are concerned with style and shape and colour.

2. Auditory

The auditory people, or hearing people, use such language as: 'I *hear* what you say', 'that *rings* a bell', 'I *hear* you loud and clear', '*unheard* of', '*word* for *word*'. When they meet you they might say something along the lines of 'I *heard* you were coming', or 'I *hear* the job's going well', and 'I look forward to *hearing* from you again'.

Auditory people, the hearing people, are concerned with sounds of all types.

3. Kinesthetic

The kinesthetic, or feeling people, use all the feeling images. For example, 'that *feels* right', 'I can't get to *grips* with that', 'let's go *hand* in *hand*', 'it just *slipped* my mind', 'let me *lay* my cards on the table'. When they meet you they might say, 'how are you *feeling?*' When you leave they might say, 'I look forward to getting in *touch* with you again.'

By now you have the basic idea that people fall into three main home-base language categories, that is visual (the seeing people), auditory (the hearing people) and kinesthetic (the feeling people).

Naturally, all of us use all the different words but tend to have this home base of language. I am sure you can *picture* the situation of a mother speaking to her small child. She says to him:

'Will you look at me when I am talking to you?'

You see the word 'look' in there. Why do we need to look at people when they are talking to us? Surely we should turn our ears towards them?

You must have heard someone say:

'It doesn't look as though you're listening.'

Again, that's the *visual* message in the language showing through.

Well, what use is this information? Why do we need to know the type of language different people use at different times? Its benefit to us in the sales profession is in building rapport, in an honest way, with our customers and clients. If we reflect back to our customers the language they are using, at a subconscious level they will feel more comfortable with our message and be prepared to listen to us more easily.

Having used this for a number of years I have found that, when you first start trying to hear people's home base of language, it takes a great deal of concentration. This can, if you're not careful, detract from hearing the other information they're providing. However, as with all things, practice does make perfect – or perhaps perfect practice makes perfect.

I suggest you play with this idea, at first with your family and friends to get yourself comfortable with listening for the clues. See for yourself, hear for yourself, feel for yourself the effect your use of reflective language is having on the people around you. Only when you become well versed in its use do I suggest you move on and build rapport with your customers in this subconscious manner.

Let us move on to discuss further what we actually say. Let me just ask you this question, 'Who did Latin at school?' Now answer this conundrum: 'Using one line make this six.'

IX

For the answer, turn the page. When I first saw this I didn't work it out either. I was conditioning your mind to think of it as a Roman numeral by the question, 'Who did Latin at school?' In fact, the technique is called 'Did you do Latin?' and this is clearly all about 'what' we say to people.

Let me ask you another question: 'Who's good at mental arithmetic?' OK, most of you are. See if you can work this one out. Imagine you are driving a bus from Luton to Watford and there is no one on the bus. At

The answer is: **S I X**

---

the first stop seven people get on. At the next stop five people get on and two people get off. At the next stop five people get on and six people get off. At the next stop two people get on and one person gets off. At the next stop ten people get on and nobody gets off. At the next stop seventeen people get on and four people get off. There are now two questions:

1. How many stops were there?
2. What was the name of the bus driver?

Yes, there were six stops and of course the name of the bus driver was your name because I started by saying, 'Imagine *you* are driving a bus.'

Could it be that the various statements we make to our customers and the various questions we ask them are preconditioning their minds to a particular thought pattern? If you go into a customer and say; 'Isn't business hard?' is it any wonder if, at the end of your sales conversation, the customer's not keen to buy your product or service? If you start your conversations with negative thoughts then that is the 'mindset' into which you have pushed your customer.

What we must be doing at the start of all our conversations is to ask a well-thought-out question or make a well-thought-out statement that will condition the conversation in a positive, professional and businesslike way.

The steps to success

Step 1

Discover which type you are, visual, auditory or kinesthetic.

Step 2

Discover which type five people you know are.

Step 3

Practise with friends and colleagues using appropriate language and reflective words.

Step 4

When you establish which type each of your customers is, make a note on your main customer records.

I am certain we would all agree that there are times when we believe our customers have fully understood what we've said. Unfortunately, in many cases this is not the situation. We must, as professionals, be constantly asking questions to ensure that the messages we are providing are understood by our listeners.

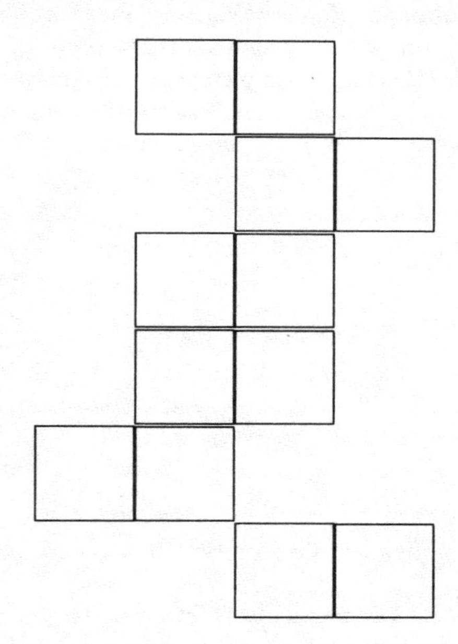

Describe the figure to a friend or colleague. They must not be able to see you nor ask any questions. The test is for you to convey information regarding the figure as accurately as possible so that the other party will end the test by drawing a figure exactly as above.

How we say it

So, not only is every single word we say important (although, according to the experts, of only 7 per cent importance) but also *how* we say things counts for much more (according to the experts, of some 38 per cent importance).

Imagine the situation where I met George in a pub, not having seen him for some five years. I walked up to him and said in a *monotone:*

'Hello, George, nice to see you again after all this time. Can I buy you a drink?'

George, I am certain, would accept the drink; however, he wouldn't feel over-excited at our meeting again after five years. But how different would be his reaction if I used exactly the same words but in an *enthusiastic* and *lively* way: I'd walked up to George, shaken him by the hand and said:

'Hello, George! Nice to see you again after all this time! Can I buy you a drink?'

We can feel instantly the difference in those two ways of speaking.

Some years ago I heard about a telephone sales course that used the word 'picture' in relation to the way in which we try to paint pictures with our voices. You will see that the word picture is written down the side of the page below. I would like you to use it as an acronym and try to find a word that begins with each of the initial letters:

P

I

C

T

U

R

E

There are no right or wrong answers; it is simply to focus our minds on a way of using our voices.

When I first heard this it was particularly relevant to telephone selling and the use of our voice on a telephone. It is equally applicable to face-to-face conversations.

For the P, I have the word . . . *pitch.* We need to decide whether or not we are going to pitch our voices high or low. The experts say the lower voice is better because it projects and carries. It is always less irritating compared to a high-pitched voice, particularly on the telephone.

For the I, I have . . . *inflection.* If we talk in a monotone, as I was when meeting George in that pub, we will bore our listeners. But if we use feelings to express an idea or mood with a rising inflection at the end of our sentences, we will be able to hold our listener's attention.

For C, I have . . . *courtesy.* In response to this question, people have often put 'clarity', which is equally important. Particularly on a telephone, common courtesy applies, as people cannot see that you are nodding in agreement with their questions or statements. During our discussion on active listening we talked about responding so that people would actually know we were actively listening.

For T, I have the word . . . *tone.* As we have already discussed, it often isn't what we say but the way in which we say it. Our voice can reflect sincerity, confidence, interest or pleasantness.

For U, I have the word . . . *understandability.* I think we would all agree that in any communication we would not talk with things in our mouth, be they cigarettes, pens, fingers or anything else. The second point with understandability is that we need to be careful with our use of jargon, slang or company abbreviations. I am sure you have found that if you are able to use jargon to build rapport with customers so that they know you understand their businesses, it can be beneficial. But if you are using your own company's jargon and the customers do not understand what you mean, they will be reluctant to ask in case you might feel they were stupid. It is very easy to alienate people by the use of inappropriate jargon.

For R, I have the word . . . *rate.* As in the speed at which we speak. If we speak too quickly people tend to listen to how quickly we are speaking. I am sure we've all heard speeches by John F. Kennedy or seen the programme *The Sky at Night* with its presenter, Patrick Moore. Both those people speak at incredibly high speeds and it can be extremely easy to start to listen to how quickly they are speaking instead of to what they are actually saying.

On the other hand, if we speak too slowly that can also be irritating because our customers will be left hanging on our every word and will try to anticipate what we are going to say and could fall into the trap of ending our sentences for us. So let's be careful with the speed of speech and make sure we vary it to make our conversations interesting.

E stands for . . . *enunciation.* The English language is full of difficulties with enunciation, particularly Ds and Ts, F and S, and P and B. Clear enunciation helps to remove misunderstandings and the need to repeat what you have said. We must be particularly careful if our products have code numbers so that our orders are clear, particularly if those orders are taken by telephone.

Let us look at the steps involved in how we use our voice and how we communicate our message.

The steps to success

Step 1

Write down some of the phrases you use regularly in your sales career.

Step 2

Read them aloud, for yourself, in a variety of styles using the ideas from the word *picture.*

Step 3

Decide how you will usually say them in the future.

Step 4

Practise out loud to the mirror or in the car.

Step 5

Smile; you'll be amazed how much impact that can have on your message.

Again, we're back to the idea that, if you do what you always did, you'll get what you always got. So if your style of speech is producing the results you want, then keep on using it; if it's not, change it.

I find one of the best ways of practising my selling voice is to read stories to the children. If you are fortunate to have children of an age when they like bedtime stories, capitalise on that opportunity to entertain the children and practise your selling at the same time.

I do believe that professionals practise and amateurs don't. If you look at any profession, be it sport or the commercial field, you'll find that the true professional does practise.

Create time in your commercial week to be involved in role-play sessions with your colleagues in order to practise the skills discussed above.

Let us now move on to that fascinating subject, body language.

Body language

Below you will find 15 different pictures and an explanation of what is actually happening in each. As usual I want to start with a test and I would like you to write down in the space provided your thoughts regarding the meaning of those body language signals.

What we must always be particularly careful about in body language is that the various signals and gestures can have a variety of meanings. We must never take a signal out of context.

Body language quiz

1. I am standing up and rubbing my hands together very *quickly*.

____

____

____

____

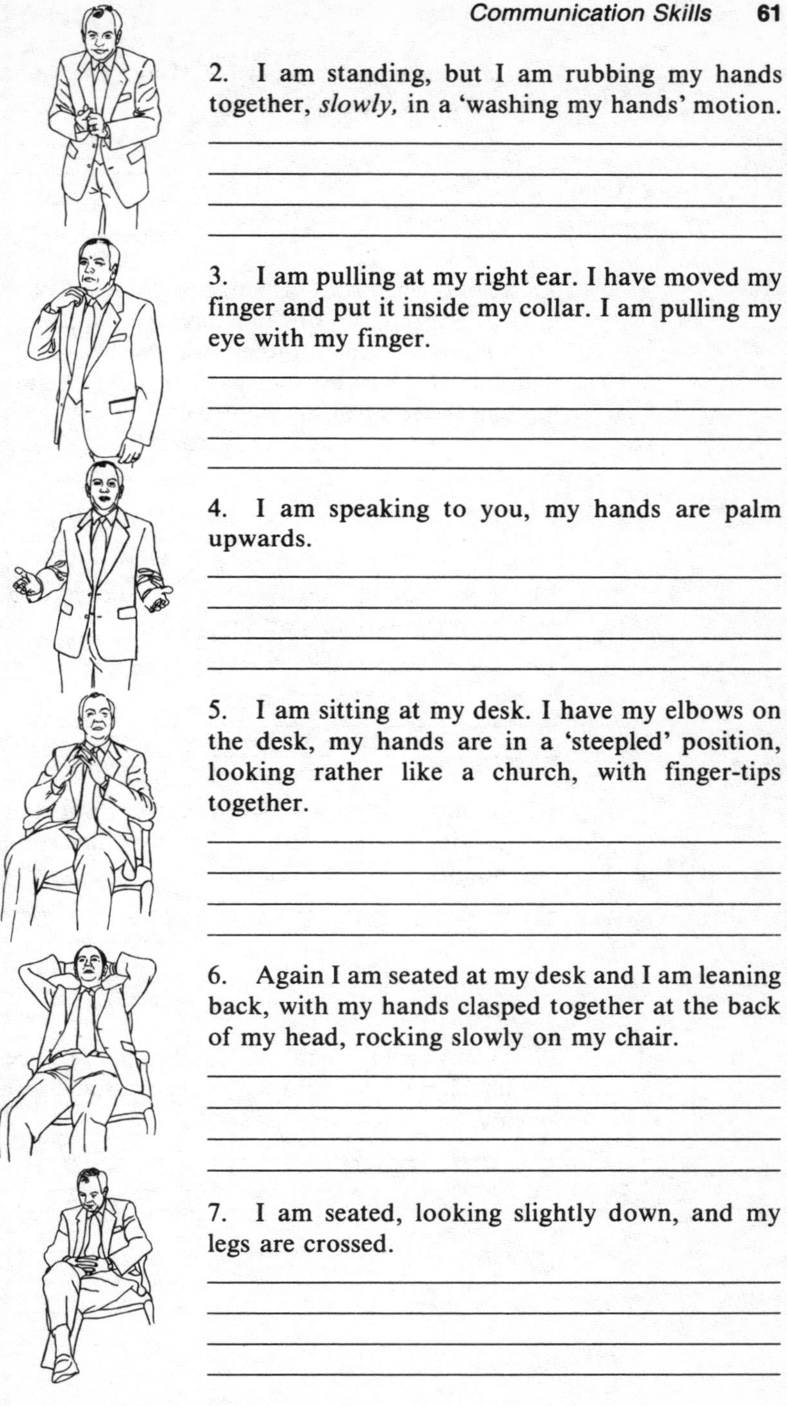

2. I am standing, but I am rubbing my hands together, *slowly,* in a 'washing my hands' motion.

3. I am pulling at my right ear. I have moved my finger and put it inside my collar. I am pulling my eye with my finger.

4. I am speaking to you, my hands are palm upwards.

5. I am sitting at my desk. I have my elbows on the desk, my hands are in a 'steepled' position, looking rather like a church, with finger-tips together.

6. Again I am seated at my desk and I am leaning back, with my hands clasped together at the back of my head, rocking slowly on my chair.

7. I am seated, looking slightly down, and my legs are crossed.

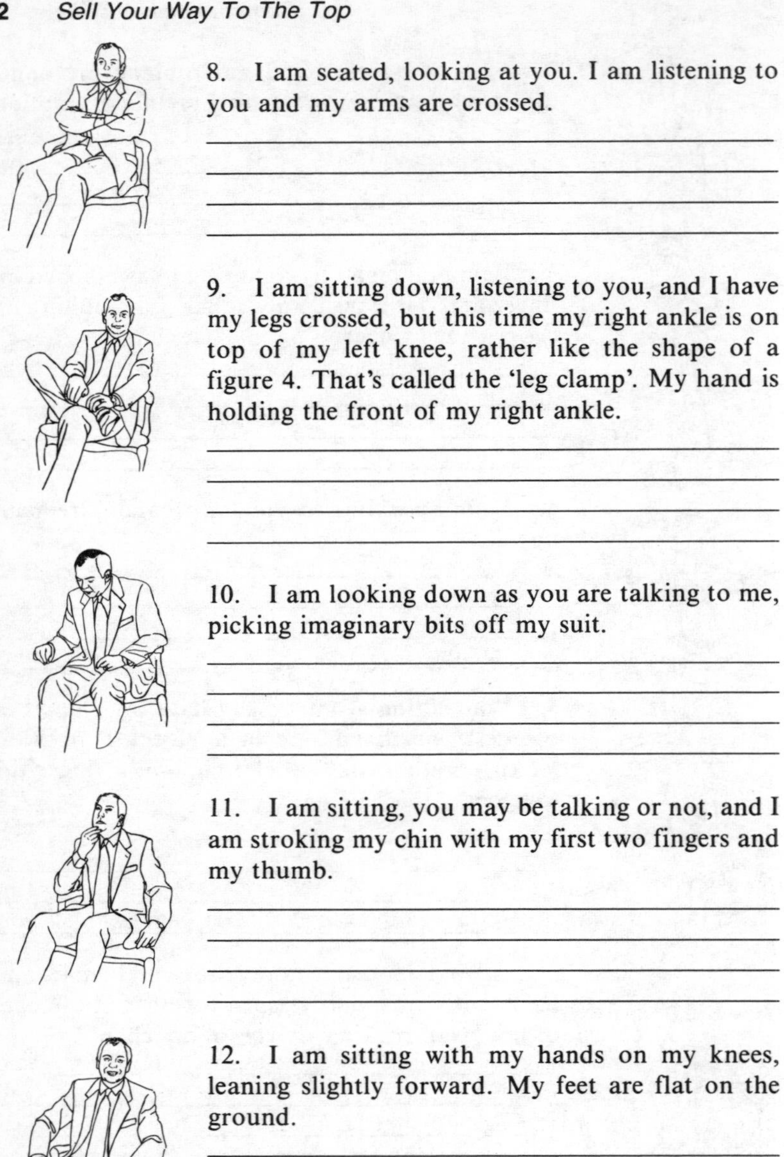

8. I am seated, looking at you. I am listening to you and my arms are crossed.

9. I am sitting down, listening to you, and I have my legs crossed, but this time my right ankle is on top of my left knee, rather like the shape of a figure 4. That's called the 'leg clamp'. My hand is holding the front of my right ankle.

10. I am looking down as you are talking to me, picking imaginary bits off my suit.

11. I am sitting, you may be talking or not, and I am stroking my chin with my first two fingers and my thumb.

12. I am sitting with my hands on my knees, leaning slightly forward. My feet are flat on the ground.

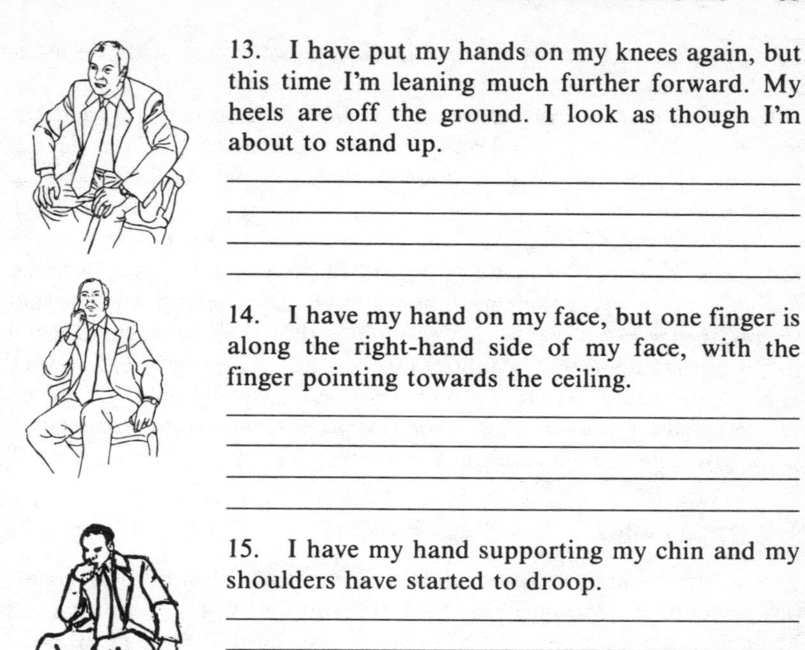

13. I have put my hands on my knees again, but this time I'm leaning much further forward. My heels are off the ground. I look as though I'm about to stand up.

14. I have my hand on my face, but one finger is along the right-hand side of my face, with the finger pointing towards the ceiling.

15. I have my hand supporting my chin and my shoulders have started to droop.

Answers

1. Fast hand rub

Now it could be that my hands are cold and I'm rubbing them together to get them warm; but it could also mean that what I am saying is good for you.

2. Slow hand rub

It could be that I have just washed my hands and found there was no towel and I am rubbing my hands together to dry them; but it could also mean that what I am saying is good for me. If I am doing this 'slow hand rub' does my verbal language reflect that it's good for me or am I trying to deceive you by saying things that sound good for you, while my unspoken truth, my body language, is giving me away?

3. Ear, eye and collar tugging

These signals, along with putting my hand across my mouth, probably mean I am lying. Of course, my collar might be too tight, my ear might be itching, my eye might be itching, but very often this will give away someone who is lying.

In old films this was used as a standard gesture to show that the crook was lying – he would pull his right eye with his finger as he was speaking. This was a classic body-language signal we all picked up unconsciously.

On this point of covering your mouth, you can spot, when you're talking to people, if they disagree with what you are saying because they will often cover their mouths while you're speaking. I know that seems strange but it is true. My thought is this: they are saying that, if they were saying it, they wouldn't like it – they would be lying. So they cover their mouths as though they were saying it. Watch for this when you are telling people things, because it is a classic signal that will show you they are disagreeing with what you say.

4. Open hands

This is easy – I am being honest. Of course, I may be putting my hands out to see if it's raining, but that's unlikely in most situations: I am being honest. Or perhaps I'm being falsely honest. You need to be careful with body language and take a number of gestures together, not just one in isolation.

5. Steepled hands

The steepled-hands position usually means I am feeling superior. Watch for this and tailor your conversation accordingly.

6. Hands behind head

This is definitely an 'I know it all' situation. I am saying to you, 'Yes, I know all about this, you can't tell me anything about it, I know it all.' Be careful you don't use it.

7. Crossed legs

This can often mean I am being negative, but not necessarily so. I might be comfortable with crossed legs.

8. Crossed arms

Again, this is a negative signal although, of course, it might be a cold day.

9. Leg clamp

This usually means I am being stubborn and I am argumentative about what you are saying. Watch out for it.

10. Imaginary bit-picker

This usually means I disagree with what's being said. Of course, it may mean I have just walked through a dust storm and am picking bits off my suit. Who knows why I am doing it?

11. Chin stroke

This is simple, easy to spot and most useful to us in a sales situation. It means I am evaluating what's being said.

12. Hands on knees, heels flat

This usually means I have come to a decision and that decision is 'yes'. Remember, though, a number of things must come into play here: it could be my eyes are open, I may be smiling, and looking excited about what has been said.

13. Hands on knees, heels raised

That's fairly obvious. I want to leave, I'm uncomfortable in the situation and fed up with what's being said.

14. Finger point

Again, this is an evaluation signal.

15. Chin support

This signal is even clearer when a closed fist supports the chin; I am saying I'm bored.

Now we have discussed a few of the many thousand non-verbal signals given by human beings to each other, let us relate this more particularly to our selling careers. The question we must ask ourselves is, 'How can we use body language in selling?'

Well, we need to be particularly observant of negative and positive body language signals. For example, if during parts of the presentation or explanation of our products or services our customers lean back with their arms folded, there is a possibility they are feeling negative about what we are saying. How will we deal with that?

My suggestion is that we change the speed of our presentation, change the emphasis of our presentation or change the style of our presentation. It may be that you can stand up if you are sitting down, or move towards the customers or give them something to hold (a brochure or the product itself). In fact, we need to do almost anything to make sure that the body language signal, if you have read it correctly as negativity, is broken.

The same would apply to the superiority or know-it-all signals – namely, the steepled fingers or leaning back, hands behind the head type of posture. At this point the customer *may* be in the wrong frame of mind to buy.

Imagine you have carefully gathered information about the customer's needs, presented your product or service to match those needs, discussed price and asked a main closing question – for example: 'Shall we go ahead then?' The customer leans forward, eyes lit up, smiling. What is the customer going to say? There is every chance the customer is just about to say 'Yes' and, in that case, what we need to do is remain silent to give the customer the chance to say 'Yes'.

I am sure there have been many instances in many sales people's careers where the customer was about to say 'Yes' and the salesperson talked for too long, discussed too many benefits and the customer changed from positive to negative.

A second situation might be that, having asked your closing question, the customer goes into evaluation mode, stroking his or her chin. The customer then leans back and folds his or her arms . . . what is the customer going to say? There is every possibility the customer is about to say 'No'. What should we do?

My suggestion is this: if you are convinced, knowing all the factors and reading the body language correctly, that the customer is definitely going to say 'No', do not let the customer say it. I am sure you have found that, once customers have entrenched themselves in a firm position, digging them out of that trench can be extremely difficult. I suggest you use what I call TOC, the Total Offer Concept, and close again. You might word it in the following way.

'Mr. Customer, before you give me your thoughts on that particular point, may I just summarise what we have discussed today?' You would then go through a list of the main benefits of your product to the customer, making sure the benefits were relevant to the customer's desires and needs. While you are giving this short, and I emphasise, short summary, look at the customer: watch his or her eyes carefully. When you have hit the 'hot button' you will know because the customer's body posture will change, his or her eyes will change and the point that created that change is the one you must emphasise.

Finishing your summary with a repetition of the major buying point, you then close again.

This method will at least give you a chance of preventing the customer from saying 'No' and entrenching him or herself in a difficult position; it will also give you a second opportunity to establish the customer's major buying motive or hot button.

There are numerous books on body language which explain the vast variety of non-verbal signals given in conversation and communication.

The steps to success

Step 1

Buy a book on body language. It is a fascinating subject and a little knowledge (while sometimes a dangerous thing), if we're careful in its application, will assist us greatly in our selling careers.

If you are involved in sales management or direction, information regarding body language is essential to the successful management of any team.

Step 2

Practise your own body language. By that I simply mean be aware of the body language signals you are giving out to your customers and ensure you do not sit in negative positions when customers are explaining their needs to you.

As we discussed in active listening, some customers do speak slowly and those of us in sales who are invariably quick minded can get impatient to move on to the next point. This impatience *must not* be communicated to the customer.

Step 3

Man watch. What I mean by this is to be aware constantly of body language and, when you are out and about in commercial and social situations, take that little bit of extra time to watch what people are doing with their bodies. You'll find it's a fascinating experience and, as with any language, the more practised you are the more fluent you become.

Step 4

Later we're going to discuss keeping records in greater detail (Chapter 16), but one of the things we should note on our main customer file is any unusual body language signals customers give. It may well be that one of your customers habitually uses the superiority gesture. Knowing that, and your strategy for disarming the situation, will be excellent information to have to hand before any sales call.

Step 5

Watch TV with the sound off. If you watch a video film (not an 'all-action' film but a dialogue film, perhaps a drama or a play) with the sound turned down, you can try to work out what is actually happening. As it's on video you can rewind it and play it with the sound turned back on to check your understanding of the body language involved. Of course, your success may be determined by the actors' ability to live the parts they are playing.

As a summary of body language, think of it this way. Imagine you were always selling . . . to a dog. When you said the right thing the dog would wag its tail. When you said the wrong thing the dog would cast down its eyes, lower its shoulders, its tail would go down to the ground and it would be obvious to anyone that it was unhappy.

Customers are just the same, they wag their tails or cast down their eyes; we simply have to be open to the signals they're giving out. Used with care, effective realisation of our customers' signals and gestures can be an immense help to our success in selling.

Let us now look at how we can read people's eyes. As with all our skills, be they NLP, rapport skills, body language skills or anything that involves watching and listening, it will take us time to become proficient. We are able to tell, by watching the customers' eyes, their degree of interest in what we are saying. The position of the eyelid in relation to the top of the eye is the indicator of interest.

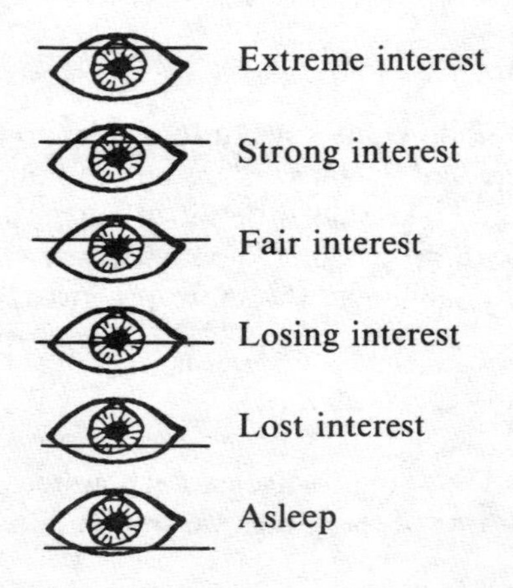

CHAPTER 7

Opening statements

There's a great expression I've known for years. Although over-used because of a shampoo commercial, it's still extremely relevant to our career in selling: 'You never get a second chance to make a first impression.'

There are three ways we usually approach our customers, be they new customers or old customers:

1. By letter
2. By phone
3. By face-to-face meetings.

The first few words we say will set the tone for the whole conversation; in fact, every single word we say or write is important. Let's have another test.

Imagine you are going to make a telephone call to a new customer. I want you to write down what you would normally say and then we'll check that opening question or statement against a list of factors that are important for this opening.

My usual opening is:

Now look down the following list of factors and give yourself one mark each time you can answer 'Yes.'

1. Did the opening break the customer's preoccupation with what he or she was doing?
2. Did the opening make the customer want to listen?
3. Did the opening excite the customer?
4. Did the opening put the customer at ease?
5. Did it make the customer feel important?
6. Did the opening set the scene?
7. Was your opening preplanned?
8. Have you previously written down your opening?
9. Have you practised it?
10. Did you obtain the customer's name before launching into your opening?

11. If you were asking for an appointment, did you have a firm reason in your mind why you were asking?
12. Did your opening statement include a benefit for the customer?
13. Did you smile while you were delivering your opening?
14. Did you sound enthusiastic?
15. Did you obtain two yesses at the start of the conversation?

I believe all those factors are important in our opening statement or question and, if you were unable to score yes for most of the questions, then perhaps we need to spend some more time on planning and rehearsing our opening.

In the space provided write yourself a new opening statement or question and then check the list again to make sure you can answer 'Yes' to most of those questions.

My new opening will be:

Let me share with you some further ideas on opening statements. We need to decide how we're going to give out our name and our company name. Are we going to say: 'My name is Bond, James Bond' or 'My name is James, James Bond?' With the first, people will probably call you Mr Bond; with the second, there is a chance they will call you James. It is obviously your decision what kind of situation you are trying to set up with the opening.

Next, are we going to say: 'I'm with . . . ', 'I'm a salesman or woman with . . . ' Again, this must not be by default. My own style is to leave out any words in between my name and the company name, so I would say: 'My name is Peter Thomson, Pinnacle Development Training.' That avoids the necessity of having a link between the two.

Here are some examples of other possible openings:

1. Giving a sample. If it is relevant in your particular business it may be you can give the customer a sample and start with: 'Mr Customer, I would like to send you a free sample of . . . ' I'm certain that word 'free' would grab the customer's attention.

2. Opening fact. We could start our openings with a stated fact, which is virtually guaranteed to arouse the customer's interest. Having created that interest we simply carry on to explain *briefly* how our product or service is relevant to the fact we have stated. You might say that based on: 'As you know . . . '

One of the methods we can use to give an opening fact is to use again our major motivators of pain and gain. The opening fact could be a pain statement, for example letting the customer know that a certain situation of potential commercial danger or difficulty is a possibility for the customer's company. Follow this with how you can solve that problem or explain a potential benefit others are enjoying and how you can help the customer experience it as well.

3. Question. By starting our conversations with an opening question we are immediately involving the customer in a buying/selling process. Such questions could start with:

'Wouldn't you agree that . . . '
'Isn't it true that . . . '
'How important is it that . . . '
'Can your present X do Y . . . '
'Isn't it your experience that . . . '
'I wonder what would happen if . . . '

4. Referral. Under the topic of telephone techniques (Chapter 15) we are going to discuss referrals, and I am sure all of us involved in the selling business would much prefer to phone a potential customer having been introduced by a current happy customer. If we are using this particular approach we will need to have planned exactly what we are going to say.

My view is that we should keep it short and simple along the lines of, 'I was given your name by . . . because . . . ' You will need to fill in those gaps to make it relevant to your business. The words that follow 'because' will relate to the benefit your current customer is experiencing with your product.

In face-to-face openings we will be able to use the two following ideas as well as the four above.

5. Shiny-object opening. All of us, whether we admit it or not, are curious and if we are able to take from our briefcases at the start of a sales meeting a 'shiny object' of some description, then the customer's curiosity will be piqued as to what this shiny object might be and its relevance to them.

Of course, the shiny object could be a brochure, a sample of the product, a plain box with the product inside it. Be as creative as possible.

6. Figures opening. Starting a face-to-face meeting with what I would term 'the figures opening' can be an extremely effective way of involving the potential customer immediately.

Simply take out your pad and pen and begin the conversation along the lines of 'Wouldn't you agree that . . . ' and start to write down figures. Then involve the customer in the mathematics of how your product or service will save or make him or her money. If it's necessary to use a calculator for these figures then, wherever possible, get the customer to do the calculations. This again will involve the customer in the process and also confirm that the figures are accurate.

7. *Call-back openings.* There are numerous times in our sales careers where it is necessary to call back on customers. This may be because we are in the regular repeat selling business and call on the same customers time and time again over the years, or it may be the situation that, on a complex sale, it is going to take a number of visits to the customer.

In either of these situations I believe we should give thought to these three ideas:

- We should always have something new and relevant to say.
- We might start with 'Last time I was here I promised I'd . . .' and, of course, you've kept your promise.
- 'You remember last time I was here you said . . .' Using the information from our carefully compiled customer records we will be able to work out an appropriate situation.

When we are checking our list of relevant factors with regard to our opening, number 15 was 'Did you obtain two 'yesses' at the start of the conversation?' My thought behind this idea is as follows.

If we are able to start our customers on the idea of saying 'Yes' as soon as possible, we have put them in a positive mood. You will recall when we were discussing 'what we say' that we talked about a technique called 'Did you do Latin?' during which I tried to precondition your minds in a particular way. If we are able to use a similar idea so that our information is received by the customer in a positive manner, this can only assist us in obtaining a sale.

How are we going to get the customers to say 'Yes'? This is actually very simple: we ask questions to which they can answer 'Yes'. How I've always done this is to say, when put through to a customer on the phone, even though I know it's Mr Bloggs: 'Is that Mr Bloggs?' The customer must surely answer 'Yes'.

I then follow it with: 'Mr Bloggs the sales director?' Of course the situation is that Mr Bloggs is the sales director and again he will answer 'Yes'. Immediately we have had two yesses at the start of the conversation, and the customer cannot help but be in a positive frame of mind because saying 'Yes' does that to your brain.

The second way we can persuade people to say yes more often is to use a method I call the 'yes tag'. All we do is to tag on to the end of any sentence one of the following expressions:

'Isn't it?' 'Didn't it?'

'Won't it?'	'Won't they?'
'Won't you?'	'Don't we?'
'Wouldn't it?'	'Shouldn't it?'
'Haven't they?'	'Hasn't he/she?'
'Can't you?'	'Couldn't it?'
'Aren't they?'	'Aren't you?'
'Doesn't it?'	'Don't you agree?'
'Wasn't it?'	

All these tags will persuade people simply to say 'Yes'. For example, 'You're enjoying our time together today, aren't you?' 'That coffee was terrible, wasn't it?', 'The hotel should provide more biscuits, shouldn't it?', 'Increasing profits is important to us all, isn't it?', 'Cutting costs involves everybody, doesn't it?'

If we can get into the habit (and like any habit it takes time to create) of using the 'yes tag', we will persuade our customers to say yes on such a regular basis they will maintain a positive attitude to the conversation.

The 'yes tag' can also be used at the start of a sentence or question, and in the middle. For example: 'Wouldn't it be nice if we could increase profits easily?' 'Shouldn't the reduction of costs be important to us?', 'If we are going to increase our turnover, isn't it true that sales training is necessary?', 'Once the computer's installed, isn't it going to make cost calculation easy?'

As with any habit it really will take practice to acquire the habit of getting people to say 'Yes'. Practise it, practise it and then practise it some more.

Let us now move on to the steps, the ways in which we can improve our opening statement and some creative ideas for those openings.

The steps to success

Step 1

We need to establish our unique selling benefit. This is sometimes called our unique selling point and, if we are able to incorporate this into our opening, then, by definition, as it is unique – it increases the chances that the customer will be interested in what we have to say.

Step 2

I suggest you write down at least 10, yes 10, new opening questions or statements, checking each time they match the 15 items or factors we've agreed are relevant. It may well be that you want to extend that list of 15 to personalise the information to your particular style.

Step 3

Dare to be different. I remember some years ago seeing an insurance consultant whom I know appear on a TV programme about his success. He was involved in the life insurance business and the local TV station crew had arrived at his home.

The interviewer turned round to him and said: 'Richard, tell me, how do you manage to focus people on the idea of talking about life insurance? Surely nobody wants to talk about life insurance? Everybody always believes they have enough life insurance.'

Richard said nothing. He simply reached into his desk, drew out . . . a grenade, pulled out the pin, held it aloft and said: 'Who has enough life insurance?'

You can imagine how that immediately focused their minds on their life insurance requirements. By the way, the grenade wasn't live, it was only a toy.

Step 4

Be creative. I heard of a man in the life insurance industry who used to attend a number of parties in London and, as always happens at social gatherings, people get round to talk about business. When asked what he did he would always say: 'I sell life insurance.' As you might imagine, most people would say in response to that, 'Oh, nice to meet you, goodbye!'

He decided to change just one word in his opening. Can you think what it was? He changed the word 'sell' to 'buy'.

When people asked what he did he would say, 'I buy life insurance.' They would respond with, 'How do you mean, you *buy* life insurance?' He would then say, 'What I do is this. I go out into the market-place, the insurance market-place, for my clients. I investigate the market and then I *buy* for them the type of insurance they want . . . would you like me to *buy* some for you?'

What an excellent and creative way to start a conversation! Having heard that idea many years ago I used it when we were in the leasing business. I would say to people when asked what I did, 'I buy money'. People would then ask me what I meant. I would simply say that I would go out into the market and buy money at the most advantageous rate in order that companies could purchase the goods they wanted. Did they want me to buy any money for them?

One of the other ideas we used at Compass Leasing plc, which was a creative solution to this potential of opening questions and statements, was the following. Having got our two yesses we would say to a customer, 'One of our major finance-house clients has contacted us because he wishes to take advantage of the tax shelter available at the end of his financial year; and he wants us to spend for him, in the next two months, £3 million. Can you help us spend it?' You can imagine how that started some excellent conversations.

Step 5

Remember to get two yesses at the start of the conversation.

Step 6

Plan *not* to do business. This may seem a strange thing to say to people involved in the selling business. However, if we make some of our first calls on customers simply fact-finding calls and then return with a full proposal, that can have a disarming and positive effect.

The insurance industry has taken this idea and now tells us that, by law, they cannot sell to us on the first visit, that they have to prepare a financial health check. Wouldn't it be excellent if we could persuade the legislators to give us that distinct selling advantage?

Step 7

Tune out the world. Whether or not we're making our first call by phone or face-to-face, it is essential we concentrate totally on the customers. We all know that it's easy to be distracted by other things happening in our own offices, when we are on the phone, or by things happening in the customer's office if we're there for a meeting.

Make sure we concentrate our total attention on the customer, on the situation and on the sales process.

Step 8

Be a shareholder. If in your business you deal with public companies, that is to say, public listed companies, then one of the great ideas I have tried is to become a shareholder in that company. It's not necessary to buy hundreds of shares, just a few. You can imagine the situation dealing with a buyer if you are able to throw into the conversation, 'I see *our* shares have gone up today.'

Suddenly the buyer is working for you. You're one of the shareholders and, therefore, one of the company's owners and, of course, you've completed a circle of business. If your product is good for your customer and will assist the customer to make profits in some way or other, as a shareholder you will ultimately benefit as well. I have tried this idea and it worked. It really did make a difference to the conversation I was having with a major client.

Step 9

Handshake empathy: in our face-to-face meetings it is usual to shake hands with the prospective customer at the start. Our handshake is not a signature; we should not have just one handshake that we use in all situations. Far better to develop an idea called 'handshake empathy', where we match the speed, the firmness and the amount of up and down movement of the other person's handshake.

This, as with all ideas, will take a degree of practice but you will be surprised at the amount of subconscious rapport you will build with your clients by using this idea.

While discussing handshakes, let's make sure we do not have the 'grip of a gorilla' in an attempt to crush the life out of our customer's hand; or the opposite, the wet-banana or wet-fish handshake that all of us hate to receive.

Use handshake empathy or what is called the 'matching grip' to reflect the type of handshake given by the customer.

Step 10

Unusual times: it is an excellent idea to make our appointments at ten to, or quarter to, the hour, instead of exactly on the hour or half hour. This will set up a situation in the customer's mind that your first visit will be short – which, of course, it may be, as there is a subconscious feeling that a meeting arranged at quarter to the hour will only last a quarter of an hour. If you are arranging for customers to call you back, ask for them to call at a specific time, for example 2.13 pm, and explain you will keep your telephone or extension open at that specific time. This again indicates to the client that you are a busy and professional person: that you value your time and, by implication, value their time.

If we spend sufficient time planning, preparing and practising our opening statement or question we will obtain more opportunities to sell and thereby increase the number of sales we make. This is an extremely important area for any sales professional; please spend as much time as it takes for you to have a powerful opening.

CHAPTER 8

Features and benefits

We're going to start another major topic, namely, features and benefits. As always we begin with a short quiz. It asks two questions.

1. What is the definition of a feature?
2. What is the definition of a benefit?

Please answer those questions now.

I believe we could describe a feature as a fact or description of the product or service we sell; we could describe a benefit as . . . what the product or service will actually *do* for the *customer*. This is an important point; it's the benefit for the customer not the benefit for us.

Customers don't buy features, they buy benefits and, perhaps more importantly, they buy *relevant* benefits. Unfortunately, a number of people in the selling profession simply tell the customer the feature and then expect the customer to go through the hard mental work of translating that feature into a relevant benefit. That is the wrong way.

What we need to do is state the feature and then go on to explain to the customers how they will benefit from that feature. We are, after all, selling results not just products. How are we going to find out the relevant benefits? Well, it's fairly simple. We need to ask lots of well-thought-out, carefully planned questions to uncover the customer's needs and wants and then we match the benefits of our product or service to those needs.

The easy way to do this is simply to state the feature and follow it with . . . and that means to you . . ., and then go on to explain how the customer will benefit and what results the customer will achieve from the use of the product or service.

The second way we are able to translate that feature into a benefit is by asking the customer a question. For example: 'How do you see yourself benefiting from this feature?' We must remember that the benefit of each feature may be different for each customer.

Suppose we look at a standard pen. If we were selling that pen in bulk to the stationery buyer of a large company the benefits would be that the pen was cost effective, that it didn't leak, that it could write in a variety of colours and, I'm certain, there are many other benefits we could think of. However, if we were selling that pen to a stationery shop or a pen retailer, there would be one major benefit and that would be the profit the retailer could make by selling that pen on to customers.

Think of it this way. The feature is the engine of a train, the benefits are the carriages following down the benefit track and the guard's van is a major motivator. You will recall that we touched on the subject of motivation and the fact that people buy because of pain, gain, crowd or proud. Within that list will be the motivator of 'peace of mind'.

Let us now examine some standard features of standard products and be aware of the benefit to a standard customer – if, of course, there is such thing as a standard customer.

Feature: The product is made on a good-quality machine.
Benefit: The benefit for the customer is that the product will be of consistent quality and the customer can have peace of mind.

Feature: The product is made from good-quality materials.
Benefit: The benefit to the customers will be that, if the customers are using the product themselves, it will last for a long time and therefore save money.

If the customer is selling this product on they will have fewer returns as it is a quality product.

Therefore happy customers, therefore repeat business, therefore make more money.

Feature: A clip on a pen.
Benefit: The benefit of having a clip on a pen is that we don't lose the pen and therefore it will save us money because we won't have to buy another one.

Feature: 1.6 litre engine in a car.
Benefit: The 1.6 litre engine will ensure the car can go faster, or give us greater prestige; or perhaps use less petrol, or be safer because we can accelerate out of trouble and therefore it will save us money and give us peace of mind.

Feature: Other people already use the products.
Benefit: The fact that others already use our products and services and we are able to prove that by our testimonial letters will give credibility to our product and to our company.

It will also generate a feeling of peace of mind within the customer, who will feel secure in purchasing. We will also be able to use this idea of the customers feeling they are part of the crowd, a crowd of knowledgeable buyers. This benefit may also relate to selling ideas and the fact that other people have already accepted the idea as feasible.

Feature: People in your company are experts.
Benefit: The customer can have peace of mind knowing that the company contains experts who are able to give advice and that the customer will receive the best service.

Feature: Your company has been in business for a considerable time.
Benefit: So often we hear salespeople saying that their companies have been established for years and at that point it really is only a feature. The benefit must be the *way* in which the company has stayed in business for a long time. Could it be because it provides a quality product or provides an inexpensive product? You must calculate why. Customers can have peace of mind in this situation.

Feature: Fast delivery or own delivery vans.
Benefit: The customers will be able to take delivery within their own specified time requirements, which will save them money, make them money or give them peace of mind.

Feature: A financial services company which uses a large number of sources.
Benefit: If the financial services company deals in money, the customer can be aware that the best possible rates of interest can be charged and therefore that can save the customer money. If it's an insurance situation, again the customer can be assured of getting the best possible arrangement.

It is totally *unnecessary* to tell a potential customer *all* the benefits of a particular product. We need to be careful that we are only selling relevant benefits. It may well be that the customer is looking for only one benefit from a product. If we are able, by careful questioning, to find out that need, what point is there in explaining yet another 15 benefits when the customer may already have decided to buy?

As another test I'd like you to work out the benefits for the following features. If you are having any difficulties at all, add the phrase '. . . and that means to you . . .' or perhaps the harder 'So what!' behind each feature. This will lead you smoothly into calculating the benefits.

What are the benefits of these features?

1. A remote control for a TV?

2. A self-winding flex on a vacuum cleaner?

3. A two litre engine in a car?

4. A snooze button on an alarm clock?

Some of the benefits of those four products may be as follows:

1. A remote control for a TV. The user can have control over which channel to watch: an important point with children in the room. It saves time. Teletext is available with remote controls. It is more convenient to be able to sit in a chair and change channel than constantly to get up and down. I am certain you can think of a variety of others.

2. A self-winding flex on a vacuum cleaner. It's safe to have a self-winding flex as the people in the house won't trip over it and therefore won't hurt themselves – a peace-of-mind situation. You can save backache because you don't need to bend down to wind the flex, you simply press a button with your foot. It's tidier to have the flex wound up and therefore our reputation will be that of a tidy person. You will appreciate with this particular one that I am going from the sublime to the ridiculous, and I'm sure you can think of still more.

3. A two litre engine in a car. Very often a larger engine will be more economical on petrol and will therefore save money. A two litre engine may have good acceleration, which can be safer in certain situations; therefore we can have peace of mind. It can give us a good image or status to have a two litre car, which we may use to attract greater business or members of the opposite sex.

4. A snooze button on an alarm clock. That few minutes' extra sleep each morning may make us better prepared for the day and therefore we will become more successful. (I don't really subscribe to this, as I think we should get up as soon as the alarm clock rings or, as some people call it, 'the opportunity clock'. If we are more physically prepared because we have allowed for that extra sleep, we will be more able to cope with the rigours of the day and therefore will become more successful, make more money and, therefore, we can die happy with peace of mind knowing that we provided for those for whom we care.

I am sure you can have a great deal of fun with this idea by seeing how many carriages you can put on the benefit track before you come to a major motivator, the guard's van.

Benefits will focus our customers on those four major motivators of gain, pain, proud and crowd. As I heard it once on an audio-tape programme from America: 'Everyone is tuned in to WIIFM,' which simply stands for 'What's In It For Me.'

Let's be aware that no one buys one-inch drill bits, they're really buying one-inch holes. No one buys matches, they're really buying flames. No one buys features, they're buying relevant benefits.

So, if you're ever unsure that the item you're discussing about your product is a feature or a benefit, ask that question, 'So what?' to yourself.

Let us now move on to the steps.

The steps to success

Step 1

I suggest you write out on cards all the features you can think of for all your products.

Step 2

On the back of those cards write all the possible benefits for different types of customers with whom you deal.

Step 3

Practise them.

Step 4

Get into the habit of saying '. . . and that means to you . . .' or an expression you create with a similar meaning.

Step 5

Increase your product knowledge because, without it, you won't know all the features and therefore cannot possibly know all the benefits.

Step 6

Ask yourself the following questions: 'How will my products or services create peace of mind for my customers?' 'How will my products or services make people feel better about themselves?' 'What problems do my products or services solve?' 'Why will my customers buy what I am selling?'

Step 7

Decide on your unique selling benefit and feature and how customers will achieve results with them.

Here are some thoughts on the possibilities of your unique selling benefit:

- Price. Might it be that you're the most expensive in the market and therefore it is of value to customers in buying the most expensive product? Or could it be that you are the cheapest in the market or perhaps provide the best perceived value for money?
- Do you make it easy for customers to buy your product? Is there an order form or a re-order form in the packing? Do you send order forms with the invoices?
- Do you provide fast delivery to satisfy the customers' need so they do not have to stock many of your products?
- The product may be easier to use than another company's.
- You offer a full money-back guarantee, which is not offered by other suppliers. This will obviously provide peace of mind.
- The product looks good and will give high esteem to the purchaser.
- There is a greater list of relevant benefits than for other products in the market-place.
- There is an exclusive feature, which is only available from you. That may simply be *you*, the salesperson.
- Your company is a great company to deal with. The people there have a positive attitude, are ready to help the customers in any way they can and generally make the buying experience a pleasure.

To summarise:

- Sell the light, not the candle.
- Sell the warmth, not the fire.
- Sell the profit, not the cost.

CHAPTER 9

Handling objections

No sales-training book would be complete without touching on the old chestnut of handling objections. This really has become a watch-word in sales, hasn't it? And yet the way in which we express this situation predetermines the way we think of the subject – as a problem.

Modern selling methods cover and handle many of the objections before they are raised by the customer. Objection handling is in reality answering questions and an objection is often the customer's indication of buying willingness.

Let's start with a short test.

1. Do I welcome objections?
2. Do I know that customers often object up to five times before saying yes?
3. Have I written down the objections I usually receive and written down a way to handle them?
4. Do I talk to my colleagues about the objections they receive and how they successfully handle them?
5. Do I have prepared but changeable ways to handle the price objection?
6. Do I regularly practise my objection-handling techniques?

If our attitude is that we welcome objections and look on them simply as customers asking questions, then I believe we will have the state of mind to answer them in the right way.

I look at it this way. Imagine I came with you on every sales call you made. Your customers only speak French, you only speak English and I am there as your interpreter or translator. When the customer says: 'Gosh, that's expensive!', you turn round to me and say:

'What did he say?'

I respond by saying to you: 'The customer said "You tell me so many exciting things that I cannot wait to buy the product now".'

Or, another example, the customer says: 'I don't like the product in blue.'

You turn round to me and say: 'What did he say?'

I respond to you with: 'The customer said: "What colours does the product come in?"'

I am certain you understand the idea. It is simply changing the way we think about customers' objections and translating them into questions we would be delighted to answer.

Customers' three main problems

Customers usually ask questions on three problems, and these are often perceived problems rather than real ones. First, they perceive a problem in changing suppliers. Second, they believe they don't need the product. And third, they believe the product to be too expensive.

Our job must be to satisfy the customer that these problems (or perhaps we should call them opportunities) can be solved.

Changing suppliers

The way to handle customers who are concerned about changing suppliers is as follows. First, compliment the customers on their loyalty to their current suppliers because that's exactly the situation we're looking for when they've changed to us. Second, make sure we go slowly because we're not likely to rush a customer into changing a supplier if this appears to be one of the customer's concerns. Third, say to the customer: 'How long have you been dealing with your current supplier?' (Possible answer . . . five years.) 'Please tell me, Mr Customer, what it was that made you change from your previous supplier to the current supplier?'

The customer's answer to this second question will clearly give you the major reasons for making the change and it may well be that those are similar reasons to why the customer might change again. You might add: 'As I know you are aware, over the last five years there have been further changes in the market-place, and I believe we are now able to offer you further benefits and reasons why you may consider making a second change.' This question will need to be customised into your particular style.

Customers believe they don't need the product

Can you recall the last time you brought a product you particularly wanted? Why did you want to buy? Could it be that your customers may have similar reasons for buying your products and their apparent lack of interest in the product is simply that you've not asked enough questions to uncover their desires or needs, and you simply haven't stoked the fire to become hot enough for them to want to buy?

We all thought we could get by without calculators. We all thought we could get by without computers, and yet today there is probably not an office in the world that doesn't have a calculator and a computer.

Can you remember when fax machines were first introduced? I am certain many customers who were approached by salespeople selling the early fax machines would have come up with the objection that they could get by without the product. Today, virtually every office has at least one fax machine.

It's too expensive

When we move into our topic about negotiation (Chapter 11) we'll talk more about handling the price question, but for the moment let's look at the reasons why a customer says a product is too expensive.

I feel it comes down to the fact that we have not made it exciting enough for the customer to want to buy. You can recall, I'm sure, having bought a car you had fallen in love with. At that point the price didn't frighten you: if you were really excited about buying it, you probably even paid slightly more than you needed to in order to gain ownership.

If we've not created that degree of desire within the customer, is it any wonder the customer is going to bring up a price objection? Using our 'interpreter', could it be that the customer is really saying: 'Show me how I can afford it.'

Some of the other ways we may answer the so-called objections from our customers are as follows. We can use a technique called 'feel, felt, found', which works like this: 'Mr Customer, I understand how you *feel.* I had another customer (name the customer) who *felt* as you do and what he *found* when he'd had our product was . . . .'

You go on to explain a success story of a client who bought your product. This is far easier to use if you have a testimonial letter from that customer, explaining how the customer was uncertain about going ahead but decided to and then, when he or she had taken delivery of your product and used it, what a success the customer had with it.

It can often pay us handsome dividends to isolate the objection by saying to the customer, having found out the reason the customer is not going to order: 'Is that the only reason you're not going ahead at this time?' If the customer is able to answer yes to that question, we can go on to say: 'If we are able to resolve that situation, will you go ahead?'

You've used the most powerful word in selling, *if,* and made the whole situation conditional on your ability to be able to answer the question.

If you've prepared the likely objections and your answers to them, you should have no difficulty whatsoever in answering this isolated situation and moving smoothly into closing for the sale.

Sometimes we come across customers who are prevaricating or procrastinating about making a decision. What we need to do is to focus on the pain of no decision and the pleasure of a decision now. Again, by having carefully calculated your possible responses in this situation, you will be able to handle it effectively.

One of the commonest so-called objections we receive is: 'I'd like to think it over.' How many times have we heard that in selling? Yet there are a variety of ways in which to handle it.

One way, and you need to be extremely careful using this, is to say to the customer: 'It's a good idea to think things over. Can you tell me where the toilets are?', to give the customer time to think it over. You leave the room for a few minutes and then come back, asking again for the order.

Second, you might say to a customer: 'Yes, I agree, it's a good idea to think things over. I do have another call in this area – what time could I come back and see you for a decision? Say, in an hour's time? Or would two hours be better?' As you will realise, in this second situation you have persuaded the customer that a decision needs to be made today and that the customer has a certain amount of time to make that decision.

Third, you might say to a customer: 'Mr Customer, in my experience when people say to me, "I'd like to think it over," it usually means that I haven't explained something properly. What is it?'

Fourth, another idea would be to say: 'Mr Customer, I agree that it's a good idea to think things over. Tell me, the thing that you wanted to think over, was it the . . .' You'll then go on to mention a feature or benefit of your product. The customer may say, 'No, that's fine, I'm happy with that', and you keep on repeating the 'Was it the . . .' until you find the real reason why your customer is not placing the order now: isolate the reason by using your 'is that the only reason' followed by 'if . . .' Handle the objection and ask again for the order.

There are three ways we can uncover a customer's real objection. Just suppose: this is a simple idea to use. You say to customers: 'Just suppose you were to place the order with me, what would make you do it?' This will make the customers tell you their major buying motives, their hot buttons; or they will respond in the negative by giving you their main objections.

A similar idea would be: 'If *ever* you were to buy this product from me, what would make you do it?' Or: 'If ever you were to use our services, what would make you do it?'

I've used this last idea on a regular basis for many years and what I usually find is that customers will ramble off in a different direction, trying not to tell you the real reason. It's often been necessary to repeat the question, 'If *ever* you were to use our services, what would make you do it?', with the emphasis on the word *'ever'*.

Third, you can try this idea: 'Mr Customer, I understand you really would like to go ahead, however . . .', and then you leave a space of silence, which the customer will usually fill in by saying: 'Well, it's a bit expensive', or 'I don't like blue' or whatever is the real objection to the customer placing the order. Again you can isolate and make the situation conditional when you are able to answer that objection. This idea, although simple to explain in a few words, is probably the most powerful way of finding out what is stopping the customer from going ahead . . . *now!*

When the relationship with your customer is right, when you have taken some time to build rapport with the customer, I am sure you will find the details are negotiable, and objections are looked on as questions. However, when the relationship is wrong and the tension is high the objections become obstacles and the customers become entrenched in their point of view.

Timing your response to the objection

When do we handle the objection?

Before it's raised

If we handle the objection before it's raised, this avoids the need to correct or contradict the customer. It allows us to phrase our objection-handling or question-handling ideas in our own way. It lets us decide an appropriate point to bring in the objections during our presentation, and it often lessens the strength of the objection as we were perfectly prepared to mention it before the customer did.

Immediately

If we decide to handle the objections immediately, I suggest we do this. It's based on a little principle called OQAC, which stands for Objection, Qualify, Answer, Close.

The customer raises an objection. We qualify the objection by asking the customer questions to make absolutely certain we understand what the customer means by the objection. We then answer the objection and we always, always, follow with a close.

I've heard sales people over the years handle an objection brilliantly and then leave a space at the end so the customer can object again. I suggest that, when you've answered an objection effectively, you ask again for the order.

Later

We should answer the objection later when it is to our advantage to leave it. However, great care needs to be taken with this. I've heard of situations where sales people have said to customers: 'I'll come to that later in my presentation', and kept on saying it to the point where the customers become so frustrated they got up and left the room.

We would also leave answering it until later if we were unable to give a satisfactory answer, or when it would mean losing control of the situation. There may be a situation where you need to refer back to someone at your company in order to provide the answer; however, great care must be taken with leaving objections because it may be they will still play in the customers' minds so they are not actively listening to the rest of your presentation regarding your product or service.

Never

There are times, albeit not many, when we can ignore the objection altogether. It may simply be raised by the customer smiling as if to present a false objection. I'm sure you've found, as I have, that customers have a habit of saying 'that's expensive' sometimes for the want of something better to say. My usual response is 'Yes', I then carry on with the rest of the presentation and questioning. If you decide not to answer some of the objections, take care – watch the customer carefully to make absolutely certain you have read the situation correctly.

The price is one of the major objections people come up with, and that we'll deal with when we discuss negotiation (Chaper 11).

Let us now move on to the steps.

The steps to success

Step 1

Write a list of the ten most common objections customers raise.

Step 2

Write them out on cards.

Step 3

On the reverse of each card translate those objections into questions and write the answers you will give to the question and the close that follows it.

Step 4

Practise them.

Step 5

Make time at your sales meetings to share information with your colleagues about objection handling.

Step 6

Maintain a positive attitude at all times towards objection handling. I once saw it written like this: '63 per cent of sales are made after the fifth objection. Of sales people, 75 per cent quit after the first objection, which is why 25 per cent of most salesforces produce 95 per cent of the business. Let's make sure we're in that 25 per cent.'

CHAPTER 10

The art of closing

Let me start our discussion on closing with this quotation: *'If you can talk . . . you can tell. If you can close . . . you can sell.'*

Have you ever wondered why companies employ people and call them salesmen or salesladies or salespersons? If a company's products are so good, if the benefits to its potential customers are so obvious, if problems never arise . . . then why do we need a salesforce?

We all know that, however good our products, however good our services, however good our ideas, it's unlikely the world will beat a path to our door to buy them. Even on the occasions when advertising or mailings bring an unexpected rush of prospective buyers, someone still needs to be able to explain the products and finally ask for the order.

Whatever business we are involved in – employed, self-employed, blue or white collar – we sell, we all sell. We sell our ideas, our products, our services or even just ourselves.

Imagine you were able to revisit all the people in your life who had said no to your proposals and, by knowing more ways to close, you were able to convert just 10 per cent more of them. How much more successful would you be today? Those proposals might have been the sale of your product or service, the sale of your ideas to your spouse, your children or your boss, the negotiation of a pay rise, the price of your new car or the cost of your house. Just the knowledge and practice of a few more closing methods or techniques, honestly used, could have saved you or made you so much money. Only you know.

Over the years much has been talked about closing techniques and there really has, in my opinion, been a great deal of misconception about the art of closing. Recently I read a brochure from a sales-training company that declared we didn't need to close. Then, as I continued to read, I realised the writer didn't mean that at all. What he meant was that we do need to close – we'll just call it a different name.

Closing has been seen as exerting pressure on people to buy things they don't really need. This must *not* be done. Pressure is totally unnecessary if the salesperson is a professional; pressure is removed altogether if the salesperson is able to explain the relevant benefits of the product concerned to a potential customer and, most importantly, to help that customer to buy. How does the salesperson help the customer to buy? How can we make it easy to buy?

It's pretty straightforward really, in fact very simple: *we ask for the order*. Let's do another test. Please answer the ten questions on closing shown below.

1. Do I understand the importance of closing?
2. Do I close often enough?
3. Do I use silence after each close?
4. Have I ever lost a sale because I didn't close enough?
5. How many people out of each ten I see say 'Yes' to my proposals?
6. When did I last learn a new close?
7. How many closes do I know?
8. How many closes do I use consciously?
9. Do I listen actively to other sales people to learn new closes?
10. Do I practise my closing skills?

Now you've completed the test, which I am sure has focused your minds on the art of closing, let me move on to share with you an amusing story I heard many years ago.

One Saturday morning a man woke up with a toothache and called a friend of his, who was a dentist, to see if he could have a look at it.

'I'm sorry,' said the dentist, 'I'm going away for the weekend, but I'll see you in my surgery at 8.00 am on Monday morning.'

'OK,' said the man, and suffered all weekend.

Bright and early our hero arrived at the surgery on Monday morning, anticipating the pain to come. He sat in the dentist's chair.

'Open wide,' said the dentist. 'Erm, it will have to come out.'

'Will it hurt much?' asked our hero, in a trembling voice.

'Not too much,' said the dentist (they always say that, don't they).

'How long will it take?' said the man, gripping the arms of the chair even tighter than before.

'Just one minute,' said the dentist, smiling a dentist sort of smile.

'How much will it cost me?' asked our hero.

'About £50,' replied the dentist, looking around for some instrument of torture.

'£50!' exclaimed our hero. 'For just one minute's work?'

The dentist smiled, paused and said, 'I can take as long as you like!'

Isn't it true that in our selling activities, whatever they may be, we need to extract that sale as smoothly, as painlessly and professionally as possible, so that our customer enjoys the experience and looks forward to the next visit to our . . . chair?

How are we going to do that? We're going to do it by closing. Many people don't close, and I believe there are three main reasons for this:

1. They don't know how.
2. They haven't practised the skills.
3. They're scared of rejection.

Well, first we need to learn as many methods, or ways to close, as possible. We need to practise those methods, customise them to our style, business and use to remove the fear of rejection by knowledge and practice and, most importantly, by having the right attitude to selling.

If we look on our discussions with potential customers as our attempt to help people obtain the product, service or ideas *they* want, then our attitude will be right.

Knowing how to close doesn't mean we pressurise our customers into buying items they don't need. Closing skills enable us to make the buying action as painless as possible. I have always found people do like to buy, but sometimes need help to make the final decision.

You know the situation, you're in a shop, showroom or office and a salesman is insistent that he explains *all* the features, *all* the benefits and *all* the variations of his product when really all you want is the necessary information for you to make a decision and for him simply to say to you, 'Do you want one?'

Over the years I have also found that people don't close because they have no belief in the product or service they are selling. I think of it in this way: *If you're not convinced, you can't convince.*

A collection of closes

We're about to go through a collection of closes I have put together over the years. I have tried all these closes in various situations and have proved they will work.

The most important point is that you will need to experiment with the closes in a role play or practice situation until you are comfortable with them and until they sound natural with your way of speaking, your product and your business. Whatever you do, don't go straight from this book and immediately try to use these closes until you have worked out precisely how they'll work for *you*!

Write down your thoughts on how to customise each one for your own use. My suggestion is that you prepare, if possible, three different ways of using each different close.

The 'if' close

We discussed earlier the power of the word 'if'. I believe it to be the most powerful word in selling. Throughout the course of your sales conversations customers will ask you questions regarding the use of your product or service. For example, 'Does this work under water?'

It would be extremely simple for those of us in selling to respond with 'Yes' and we could have a lengthy conversation with every customer constantly 'giving away the yes'. My suggestion is this: stop saying 'Yes' and start saying 'If'.

When a customer asks, 'Does it work under water?', respond with something along the lines of: 'Would you like it to work under water?' Or: 'Is it important to you that it works under water?' The customer will say 'Yes'. Then you would be able to say: '*If* I am able to arrange it so that the product will work under water, would you like one?'

You will realise that this brief explanation sounds somewhat gauche, but I'm certain you will be able to take this idea and, by careful thought, blend it into your responses to customers' questions.

Some years ago in the early days of car telephones, I sold car telephones, and the coverage area was somewhat limited (albeit the service was being provided by British Telecom). This was in the days of the early 'push to speak' type telephones, with a limited number of channels on which telephone calls could be made.

Customers would say to me: 'Peter, does the phone work in Liverpool?' Knowing that if I said yes I would then be into a list of all the towns in the country, establishing whether or not the carphone worked there, I would always respond with, 'Do you want it to work in Liverpool?', to which the customers would usually, but not always, respond with, 'Yes'.

I would then say, with a smile on my face, 'If it works in Liverpool, do you want one?'

Very often the customer's reason for this initial question was that the customer visited that area on a regular basis, and the major use of the carphone was going to be when the customer was away from the office in that area. Little further conversation was needed regarding the use of the phone if we'd already established a solution for this primary problem.

You might use this powerful word 'if' in the question: 'If ever you were to order, what would make you do it?' Again, this may uncover some major buying motives.

Use this rebounding technique of not saying 'Yes' but saying 'if'. First, make sure the question has some relevance in the customer's mind and, second, it will give you a marvellous closing opportunity.

You might use this 'if' close with the children when they ask for sweets by responding with, 'If you can have sweets, will you do the washing up?' You'd be surprised how easily that will work for you.

The 'straight' close

The 'straight' close is as easy as asking for the order, by using such simple ideas as: 'Shall we go ahead then?', 'Please may I have the order?', 'Will you order one?'

You already have this idea and can work with it to find words that are comfortable for your use.

The 'alternative' close

This is probably the best-known close in selling and is simply a matter of suggesting to the customers that they take one of two choices. The beauty of the close is that it assumes the sale and that the customer's only decision is not whether to buy but which alternative to buy.

You can use it with colours (for example: 'Do you want the red one or the black one?'), with delivery ('Do you want delivery next week or the week after?') or with the number of products ('Do you want three of these, or six of these?').

There are so many ways to use this you could go through almost every factor of your product and its service to the customer and work out an alternative for each one.

The 'non-alternative–alternative' close

I developed this idea many years ago, having read that Henry Ford had said his cars were available in any colour as long as they were black.

You will need to pick your situation carefully to use this particular close, as it is certainly light hearted and needs to be said with a smile, in the right situation, to the right customer. The way I used it was as follows.

Going back to the days when I was selling carphones, I would say to the customers:

'Wouldn't it be a nice idea if you could have a carphone that matched the interior colour of your car?'

Customers would invariably respond with 'Yes'. I would then say:

'Carphones come in four colours, black, black, black or black. Which one would you like?'

On every single occasion when I used this close with a broad smile on my face, the customer would say, 'I'll have the black one!' I'd say 'Great' (and really meant it), take out my order pad and the business was concluded.

Are there situations in your business where you can use this idea, carefully picking your moment?

The 'enough' close

'Enough' is one of those little words in the language which, although only six letters long, can be tremendously powerful in a selling situation.

When I was first in my selling career I worked for an American company called Diversey, selling cleaning chemicals to the catering industry in Herefordshire and Worcestershire. One of our products was an excellent detergent called 'Tig', which came in five-gallon drums. I would say to customers, having discussed the relevant benefits and its cost-saving to them, 'Do you think that the six drums will be *enough*?'

Of course, if the customers said 'Yes', I then had an order for six. If the customers said 'No', they wanted more than six.

How many ways could you use the enough close? With delivery, with volume, with colours – so many different ways.

The 'minor point' close

We use the 'minor point' close to obtain the customers' agreement to a minor point concerning the sale – by which agreement they have agreed to the whole sale. For example: 'Will you need the A3 paper-feed with your new copier?' If the customer says 'Yes', he or she is obviously thinking very strongly about buying the copier. Why else would the customer be agreeing to have an A3 paper-feed?

What minor points of your product or service can you close on in order to move customers down the road of agreeing the whole sale?

The 'hurt and rescue' close

This close is used by companies throughout the world, but we usually don't even spot it happening. What sales people are doing is frightening us with their first statement or question and then rescuing us with a softer option. For example, in response to a price for your second-hand car from a second-hand car dealer, the salesperson might say: 'I think it's worth about £500.'

The look of horror on your face clearly indicates that you have been hurt. You might be rescued with: 'Oh, no, perhaps I could give you £750 for it.'

When I sold carphones I would say to customers, again in a jocular fashion (remembering by now I'd built a good relationship with the customer because of the conversation we were having): 'We're going to fit an aerial to the back wing of your car' (these were the days before hand-held phones) 'and we're going to need to drill a hole in your wing about this big.' I'd hold my hands up showing a hole of some four or five inches in diameter.

The customer would look with horror at this idea. Smiling sweetly, I would respond with: 'I was only joking. It's about this big. That'll be OK, won't it?' (Holding up my first finger and thumb, showing a hole of approximately half an inch in diameter.)

'Phew,' the customer would say, 'that'll be fine.'

When you're being sold to, watch out for this idea. You'll find it's used extensively. How many ways could you use it with your products?

The 'ownership question' close

This is sometimes called the 'assumptive close', and it works as follows. If we ask the customer questions based on their having already ordered the product in question and, having taken delivery, they are using the product, moving them past the point of sale will be extremely simple.

For example, imagine you are selling a copying machine and the customer has a two-floor office block. You might say: 'Will the downstairs staff also be using the copier?'

If the customer says 'Yes', the customer is already picturing the copier in use; if 'No', the customer is still picturing the copier in use but there may be an opportunity for a second sale.

There are without doubt numerous questions you can ask your customers regarding their use of the product and, properly phrased, as though a sale had already taken place, this will assist the sale to go through. Do not ask questions based on the possibility of the customer ordering – ask questions based on the fact that the customer has already ordered.

The 'oh, well' close

I heard this close on an audiotape many years ago, and have tried it and found that the idea is extremely easy to use and extremely effective. It works as follows. You ask the customer a question regarding the time-scale of ordering or using the product. For example: 'When were you thinking of placing the order, in three months' or six months' time?' 'When were you anticipating delivery, a week or three weeks' time?' Or some similar question.

After the customer's reply, you respond with: 'Oh, well, we'd better get the paperwork sorted out today,' smoothly taking out your order pad.

As with all these closing ideas, you need to be careful in their use and make sure you are using them with the customer's benefit in mind: using them honestly and using them smoothly and professionally. The whole purpose of closing the sale is motivation, not manipulation.

The 'similar situation' close

We have already discussed, in handling objections, how to use 'feel, felt, found'. The similar situation close explains another client's success story, preferably allied to a testimonial, with the particular words: 'I understand how you *feel.* I had another customer who *felt* that way, but what that customer *found* was . . .'

The 'testimonial' close

In my opinion, all of us in selling should have testimonial letters that we are able to use in future sales conversations. These letters are extremely easy to obtain . . . ask for them.

I have hundreds of testimonial letters from those who have attended training courses or heard my audiotape programmes, and I use them to prove to other people that the training will work and be profitable. I have different testimonials from different types of client.

My suggestion is you contact your major clients who are happy with the services and products you supply, and ask them to write to you indicating their pleasure. If they are having difficulty phrasing the letter to you, write the letter out you want them to send you and ask them to adjust it as they see fit.

How do we use the testimonial close? Imagine you're with a customer who is keen to move ahead, but just can't make that final decision. You might say:

'Mr Customer, if I was able to bring into this room six other managing directors' (for the sake of this discussion we're talking to a managing director) 'and they were able to say to you they had tried the product and were extremely happy with its use, would you believe them and go ahead?'

Most customers in response to this will say 'Yes'.

You respond with: 'Well, as you will understand, it would be extremely difficult for me to arrange for six people to attend here all at the same time. However, what I do have is letters from six of my customers confirming that the product (or service) did live up to their expectations and that they are delighted with it.'

Pass over your testimonial-letters file. These letters need to be in clear plastic wallets so they don't become damaged, and they must be on the original company letterheads. Photocopies should be avoided if at all possible.

At this point, and I'm sure you'd agree with me, customers do *not* read carefully any volume of written information while somebody else is in the room. They 'skip' read it.

What I *always* do when I pass my testimonial collection to the customer is to make some excuse to leave the room for a few moments. This might be as simple as a request for the location of the toilets, some reason to go back to your car or any other reason.

Whatever you do if you're using the testimonial close, leave the customer alone to have the time to read the testimonials properly. That way you have a greater chance of success.

I have found that if, on my return to the office, the customer is still reading the testimonials, it is virtually certain an order will be placed. If the testimonial file is closed and the customer is on the telephone talking to somebody else, I know I have more work to do.

Make a note *now* on your action plan for the art of closing that you *will* contact your customers to get testimonial letters.

The 'impending event' close

We all know this close and I am certain it's been used on all of us at some time in our commercial lives. It is as simple as contacting our customers and letting them know of some impending event that will change the factors relating to our product or service.

It might be a price increase, it might be a change in the rate of value added tax. It might be that your company is about to be taken over, and deliveries are going to be from a different place. Whatever *truthful* impending event can alter your situation can be of advantage to you to persuade prevaricating customers to order. If you have customers who nearly ordered in the past, contact them again when you have a truthful impending event to share with them.

The 'puppy dog' close

The puppy dog close is based on the old idea of a couple going down to the local pet shop with their children one Saturday morning. The children, Johnny and Mary, want to buy a puppy. Mum and Dad aren't so certain and so the pet-shop owner gives them the dog and simply says: 'Take him home for the weekend and bring him back on Monday morning if you don't want to keep him.'

I think this is a risky proposition – you never know what the dog might do to and in the house. However, it has obviously worked as it's still used today.

I know that Mercedes-Benz car dealers use this idea and, if they believe you are a serious purchaser, they will lend you a Mercedes for a weekend so that you fall in love with it and won't want to go back to your old car.

The growth of multi-level marketing companies throughout the world has seen one of the major companies, NSA, use the puppy-dog close idea with its filtering products. A dealer in NSA water filters will lend you a water filter for probably seven days or more. By the time you've got used to filtered water as opposed to chlorinated tap water, you are certainly well motivated to keep the product.

Is it possible one of your products, or part of one of your products, could be lent to one of your customers on a trial or puppy dog basis?

The 'Benjamin Franklin' close

The Benjamin Franklin close or, as it's sometimes called, the 'Winston Churchill' close (although I don't know why) is extremely easy to use. It is a matter of drawing a line down the centre of a page to create two columns and labelling those columns either 'for and against' or 'plus and minus'.

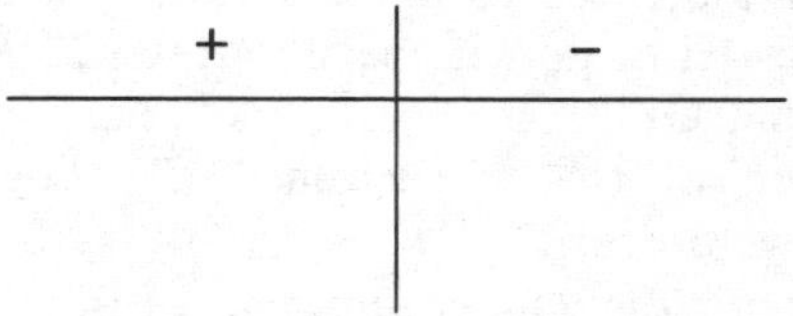

You say to a customer who is hesitating to make a decision: 'Mr Customer, might I suggest as we are close to finalising our arrangements that, in order to make sure we are moving in the right direction, we take a balance-sheet approach to the idea and list the "fors" and "againsts" for going ahead today?'

You then list in the 'for' or 'plus' column all the positive points, all the benefits for the customer placing an order today. As you have been asking careful questions and listening actively to the answers, and watching the customer's body language, you will be well aware of what the hot buttons are and should be easily able to list at least ten points why the customer should proceed.

You next pass the piece of paper and pen to the customer, and leave the customer to fill in the 'minus' or 'against' column.

Whatever you do, do not assist customers to fill in the minus column. This must be the point at which the customers take control of their own destinies. If you add the phrase, 'and you can be the judge' when explaining the method to the customer, you will remove all the pressure – which we all know is the right thing to do.

On the few occasions I have used this close, it has been extremely effective and, by the time the customer has written down three 'against' or negative reasons, he or she has turned round to me and said: 'Peter, I see what you're saying. Let's go ahead.'

To be able to use this close you need to have a list of all your product's benefits, which you may have ticked as being relevant to the customer during the course of your questioning stage.

The 'think it over' close

This is a closing opportunity all of its own, and we have talked about this in our discussion concerning handling objections. We go down a list of 'Was it the . . .' and then isolate, handle the objection and close again.

The 'test' close

This is also called the 'temperature' close, and it can be used in three different ways.

First, it is a simple check to make sure the customer agrees with what we are saying: 'How do you feel about that?', 'How do you think about that?', 'Is that OK?'

Second, we can say to the customer: 'Do you have any other questions before we proceed?'

And third, by using the temperature part of the close, we say to the customer: 'On a temperature scale of 1 to 10, how hot are you at the moment about going ahead?' I have found on every single occasion I have asked this question that customers have always said 'six'. I don't know why that has been the case, but it always has been.

You respond with: 'What do I need to do in order to increase your temperature to 10?'

The customer, usually, will tell you. You follow that with 'If I', repeating back to the customer the necessary factors to increase the temperature to 10, ie., the point at which the customer will place the order . . . 'You'll go ahead, then?'

You've clearly asked the customer what you need to do to get him or her to place the order. The customer has told you, you've made it conditional, and now all you need to do is satisfy the conditions the customer has laid down.

The 'corridor' close

This close has also been called, over the years, the 'ascending' close, and recently I heard it called the 'hem of the skirt' close. My original idea was to think of a sale as moving down a long corridor with the customer, closing a series of doors behind us on all the relevant points regarding the product or service.

We would only shut each door when we were absolutely certain the point in question was relevant to the customer, that we had clearly explained all the benefits of that point, and that the customer had agreed that the facts being discussed were of interest to him or her and that the benefits were relevant.

While using this close you could write down each benefit as the customer agreed them, or each feature or factor and place a reasonably large tick at the side so that the customer was not able to retreat to a particular point later in the conversation when you ask for the order.

During a sales-training course for a major printing company in the UK, one of the salesmen said to me that he'd always known this close as the 'hem of the skirt' close. This was based on the fact that, if someone hemmed a skirt with one long piece of thread, at any point along that hem the thread could be cut and the whole hem would fall down. If, however, each stitch was tied off, it was unlikely the whole repair would run – it would be simple to repair each stitch. The way you would be able to hem the skirt or shut the door is to use the 'yes tag' we discussed earlier.

The 'sudden death' close

The sudden death close should be used with great care and only when it has become apparent that you really have reached a stalemate with the buyer.

As a final attempt you could turn round to the customer and say: 'Mr Customer, either this is a good idea and we should go ahead now, or it isn't and we should forget it. Tell me, which is it?'

You will realise the power of this close and that it could go either way. If it goes against you, it is my belief the chances are that you wouldn't have obtained the order anyway. Take care in using it: it really is a blunt approach.

The 'order form' close

The idea of completing an order form while going through a sales conversation is extremely old and has been used by salespeople for many years. I believe, however, we need to be extremely subtle in its use, as taking out an order form at the start of a conversation and filling it in as the customer answers our desire-finding questions could easily prompt a response such as: 'What do you think you're doing, I haven't placed an order!'

However, used at the right time, which may be well into the

conversation, it can be very powerful and set up the situation in the customers' minds that they really are going to place an order today.

On this point about order forms, if it is necessary in your business for you to have a customer sign an order form, then please use the following. (I know you will consider this to be a hard-line approach, totally contrary to the ideas put forward by most sales trainers.)

When you want the customers to sign the order, ask them to *sign* the order. Do not ask them to 'OK' it or 'jot their name just here'. I have found that customers who sign orders, *knowing* they have signed an order, do not cancel. Customers who have 'OK'd' a piece of paper or 'jotted their name' on a piece of paper are far more likely to have second thoughts and cancel.

This is based on the fact that any difficulty in a sale – and signing an order can be a difficult point for a customer – should be handled clearly, honestly and without frills.

If the customer is signing a lease for five years for a new copier, fax machine or computer, do not fudge round the fact that the lease is five years long. Say it loudly and clearly in response to the customer's question, 'How long is the lease?' I always used to say when I was in the leasing business, 'The lease is for . . . five . . . long . . . hard years. Please sign here'. Customers would invariably laugh and still sign.

Putting your hand over your mouth and mumbling 'five years' will have the customer wondering whether or not the term is too long.

Similarly, when asking a customer to sign, why should we wish to make it any easier than 'Please sign here?' My personal view is that it is a weak approach to ask a customer to 'OK' something. Please don't do it.

The 'Columbo' close

You'll no doubt have seen the TV series with the detective in the scruffy mac called Lieutenant Columbo. The technique he uses is to ask his suspect a series of questions, which are not always overly relevant. Having reached the door on his way out, with his subject in a relaxed mode thinking Columbo is leaving, he turns round, one finger tugging at his eyebrow, and asks his main question. His subject is relaxed and gives away more information: the key fact.

The way we can use this when we are selling is as follows. Imagine you have been through all the needs analysis with the customer. You have presented your product properly, clearly explained the relevant benefits, and the customer has seemed interested but, despite all your skills, you cannot get the customer to buy. Standing up and closing your case, you thank the customer for their time. You shake the customer warmly by the hand (not by the throat) and move towards the door.

As your hand reaches the door knob, in order to open the door to leave, you turn round to the customer and simply say: 'Tell me, Mr Customer, what was the real reason you didn't go ahead today?'

At this point the customer will have relaxed, knowing you are going, knowing he or she has succeeded (or so he or she believes) in resisting your charm and the benefits of your excellent product. In this relaxed state, the customer will invariably tell you the real reason he or she didn't proceed. You turn, march smartly back to the customer's desk, and say: 'Oh, I obviously didn't explain that very well. What I meant to say was . . .' And you go on to cover that major objection.

If we had the strength to use the Columbo close on every occasion where the customer did not order on the day, I believe we would dramatically increase our sales and thereby dramatically increase our earnings. You may even be able to use the Columbo close over the phone.

When we are honestly selling an honest product that will benefit our customers, it is our job as salespeople to close as many orders as possible. That's why we're employed. We all know the situation where we have bought products, over the years, about which we knew nothing until a salesperson called to see us, or a piece of advertising or letter aroused our interest. That's the purpose of being in the sales business, to bring the ideas of our products to all the potential customers we can.

The 'invitational' close

The invitational close is again to be used with customers who simply won't make up their minds. Ask this question: 'Mr Customer, why don't you give us a try?'

What could be simpler? A softly spoken question, 'why don't you give us a try?', will often move the most hardened buyer.

The 'take away' close

I hear this close so often when I ring companies to order products. Knowing you want to buy, they respond with: 'Let me just check if it's in stock.'

That fear of loss can, if you're not strong, take away any thoughts of negotiating the price. I once knew someone who sold personalised car registration plates, and who used this idea on a regular basis. When anyone ever phoned about a car number-plate he would always say (though it was not the truth): 'I think it's sold.'

I'm not suggesting for one moment you tell lies to the customers. There might be situations within your company where it is necessary for you to check that 'it's in stock', or that a machine has a particular capacity to meet the customer's order.

This fear of loss is a major motivator for us all.

The 'approach' close

This close is to be used at the start of a sales conversation and is phrased along the following lines: 'Mr Customer, I will show you why others have bought our product; will you please look and then tell me either yes or no?' What you've done by asking this question is to focus the customer's mind on the fact that he or she has to give you a decision at the end of your demonstration or presentation. Wouldn't it be a great situation if we knew that, after every demonstration, the customer would decide?

Perhaps by using the approach close, after we have practised it, we can create that situation for ourselves.

The 'invalid assumption' close

I have included the invalid assumption close because I have heard of it and heard of people using it. I do not use it myself and must admit I'm not over-comfortable with its use. It works as follows.

By listening carefully to the customer, and picking up one fact relevant to the sale, we repeat that fact back to the customer, changing the information slightly.

If the customers are keen to go ahead, they will correct our invalid assumption and thereby confirm their desire to buy. For example, during the course of a conversation you have heard a customer say they are looking for delivery of a product by the 15th of the month. In summarising the conversation, the salesperson says: 'And of course you must have delivery by the 25th.'

The customer responds: 'Oh, no, we must have it by the 15th.'

The 'mathematical extension' close

The mathematical extension close or 'reduction to the ridiculous' close is the one to use when the price has become a problem. To use the close effectively, we must have calculated before meeting the customer all the figures involved. Let me explain it.

Very often the total price of your product can frighten the customer. If we are able to break the price down to a minor amount over a relevant 'use' period, this can make it easier for the customer to buy.

For example, you sell a machine that costs £5,000. The machine will last the customer a minimum of five years. The customer makes a product with this machine. You could explain the cost as follows:

Question: 'What is the retail price of the product you will make on this machine?'
Answer: '£3 each.'

Question: 'How many per hour will the machine make for you?'
Answer: 'Four.'

'Mr Customer, this machine will cost £5,000 and will last a minimum of five years. That's £1,000 a year before tax relief. Say, £20 a week and, over a 40-hour week, about 50 pence per hour. Surely, Mr Customer, to get sales of £12 (4 × £3) you can afford 50 pence per hour, can't you?'

I'm sure you can see clearly how we could use this idea of reduction to the ridiculous with almost any product, and I always suggest that the calculation is done aloud so the customer knows for certain where the argument is leading.

To use this close effectively you must have practised the mathematics involved so you know how to do it smoothly – but it still can be extremely powerful in presenting the price of your product.

Let's say, for example, that you sell print. The printing business is extremely competitive and very often good-quality printers are losing orders that are based purely on price. Is it that we're comparing the price of the whole print-run to another printer's price or are we breaking down the price per sheet so that the difference is fractions of a penny? We could explain clearly to the customer the additional benefits of dealing with our company, which would 'surely be worth' those additional fractions.

If we're talking about the profits a customer is going to make with our product or service, we need to gross it up. If we're talking about the costs, we need to reduce it to the ridiculous.

Silence

We have reached the end of the list of closes but, as I am sure you will realise, I've not forgotten to include a discussion about the most important point of . . . silence. All of us involved in selling have heard of the idea that we need to use silence after we have closed, and I totally agree with that. For those of you who may be new to this, the idea is simple. Having asked a closing question we need to give the customer time to make a decision, and therefore we need to *shut up*. If we interrupt while the customer is evaluating our question, we may well have interrupted a 'Yes'.

Many buyers understand the pressure or power of silence, and will often keep a salesperson hanging on simply to take control of the situation. The old idea was that whoever spoke first, lost. Fortunately, there is yet another technique to overcome this pressure when it becomes too great. This is what to do.

When, and only when, the length of the silence has become so difficult it is beginning to destroy the rapport you have built with the customer, lean forward towards the customer, first looking left and right in a conspiratorial sort of way, and in a quiet voice and with a smile say: 'My mother always told me that silence meant yes. Is that the case here?' Having used this technique on a few occasions, I found the customers always, always, laughed and said . . . '*Yes*'.

As always you will need to practise this with your colleagues or perhaps in a mirror so that you can use it with great effect.

Committees

Here are some thoughts about dealing with committees. Don't give out too many brochures: you'll find that the members of the committee will read the brochures and won't listen to what you are saying. Make sure you get the names and titles right, and write them down. Maintain eye contact with the various members of the committee. If one person seems very interested in what you are saying, use them as the responder to your 'yes tag'.

Go slowly. There's always one member who moves at a snail's pace. That member might just have the casting vote. Always finish on a list of benefits and, perhaps, with the line: 'Well, I'll leave you for a few moments so you can make the final decision.' Always send a follow-up letter thanking the committee for their time and summarising the main benefits again.

Let's now move on to the steps for the art of closing.

The steps to success

Step 1

Get testimonial letters.

Step 2

Write out the closes we've discussed on cards, and your personalised use of the closes on the back of the cards.

Step 3

Practise them before you use them with the customers.

Step 4

As you use the cards, during the course of your selling career, keep notes on them as to which closes work for you, both in style and content.

Step 5

Get into the habit of closing with friends and colleagues, just for fun. As I said at the start of this chapter, if you can talk you can tell. If you can *close,* you can *sell.*

Only ever use these closing ideas and techniques to sell your products honestly to a customer who you know will benefit from their use.

If you persuade people to buy things that will only involve them in cost and not profit, this will eventually rebound on you. Our success is simply a by-product of our customer's success.

Use these closing ideas to make your customers more successful and *you* will become more successful.

CHAPTER 11

Negotiation

I could say that negotiation is a very tricky thing, particularly when we are selling as our success or failure is determined by the way we negotiate and the results we obtain. Or I could say that negotiation is easy and simple to do and, if we follow some basic rules, it's so much fun.

The difference is in our attitude towards what we are doing. If we enter into negotiations believing there are going to be problems, then there probably will be. If we enter into negotiations believing we're going to be presented with opportunities, that's probably what will happen.

The major part of this chapter is going to be taken up with a quiz. Some years ago I read an excellent book that I can highly recommend to you: *Everything is Negotiable* by Gavin Kennedy. I have used some of Gavin's ideas together with my own experiences in order to prepare this quiz. I'll give you multiple-choice answers so that all you have to do is to decide on A, B, C, D or E.

The quiz

Question 1

You have decided finally to get rid of your vintage car, and you would be well pleased if someone would pay you £30,000 for it. You have telephoned your advertisement to a national newspaper and, before the advertisement appears, someone from the local vintage-car club approaches you and makes you an offer of £32,000 in cash immediately. Do you

A Ask your potential customer to wait until the advert appears?
B Haggle?
C Take the £32,000?

Question 2

You want to buy a speedboat and you see one advertised with a trailer and a load of other goodies at £11,000. You know that, if you're extremely careful with your budget through the next few months and use that small bank loan the bank manager promised you, you could raise approximately £9,500.

You meet the owner of the boat at the local marina where the boat is moored. In dicussion you mention that you would be able to find, with difficulty, the £9,500. The owner offers to sell you the speedboat with the trailer and goodies at this price. Is this

A An occasion to phone your spouse with the good news and instructions to put the champagne on ice?
B As the godfather would say in the Mario Puzo films, 'an offer you can't refuse'?
C An awful position?

Question 3

You operate your business from a rented factory and you know that, in the very near future, the landlord (with whom you have only a handshake agreement) is going to be looking for an increase in the rent of some 30 per cent. Do you

A Write to him immediately, explaining all the problems you are having with the building and the fact that you want the problems solved?
B Ask for a reduction in the amount you currently pay in rent?
C Make an offer of 15 per cent increase?
D Suggest you take the discussion to a rent tribunal so that they may arbitrate?

Question 4

You run a small business and have been extremely busy manufacturing your product range. You have arranged to deliver the products to your major customers during the coming weekend. On Friday morning your delivery van breaks down.

The owner of a local business has a similar van and offers to let you use it for the weekend, asking you to sign a piece of paper that says simply: 'The rental of one vehicle for the weekend of the 17th and 18th, cost £100.' Do you

A Insist that, as it's a business matter, you need to have a contract drawn by your solicitors, or your joint solicitors?
B Sign as requested?
C Suggest that, as you know each other and are both local businesspeople, a receipt isn't necessary?
D Ask for more information?

Question 5

You make widgets and, after trying to get an appointment for many, many, months with the buyer of a large company, the buyer finally phones you. He says he has a few minutes to spare and is in your town. He asks to meet you at the local airport where he is flying off for six weeks to visit one of the other factories in his company's group. This seems to be a marvellous opportunity.

In a brief five-minutes meeting at the airport, the buyer asks you for your best price for a six-months contract to supply Mk III widgets. What do you do?

A Quote a high price in order to leave yourself room to negotiate at a subsequent meeting?
B Quote a price just above your best price?
C Quote the lowest possible price in order to start the relationship?
D Give him your best wishes for his trip?

Question 6

You're negotiating with the buyer of a reasonably large company. When you've told the buyer the price of your product, he says: 'You'll have to do a bit better than that, the competition is extremely strong.' What do you do?

A Ask what the difference is between your price and the other prices?
B Tell him that, if he gives you the order, you'll cut the price?
C Ask what he likes about your particular proposal?
D Tell him you'd like to see the other offers?
E Tentatively suggest that if the others are that good he ought to accept them?

Question 7

Your computer system is running extremely well but you are concerned about being exposed to only one machine. You're going to buy a new computer with a laser printer and all the bells and whistles.

A local, regular supplier has quoted you £5,400. What size discount do you expect to get?

A 20 per cent?
B 15 per cent?
C None?
D 5 per cent?

Question 8

You are a toy washing-machine salesperson and you receive a telephone call asking you to go to a day nursery run by the local council. The matron in charge of the nursery says she wants to buy one of your toy washing-machines. This has a retail price of £1,800 plus VAT.

The matron explains she has to work to her budget, which is decided by the county council, and she is unable to spend any more than £1,600 plus VAT. What do you do?

A Tell her the deal is not possible and leave?
B Ask her to keep your arrangements strictly secret and discount the price to £1,600 plus VAT?
C Explain the relevant and *missing* benefits of a machine that's priced at £1,575 plus VAT?

Question 9

A man is walking across the desert leading six camels. He arrives at an oasis. At the oasis is another man who has a sign that says 'Water, price one camel'. Who has the 'power' in the negotiation?

A The man with the camels?
B The man with the water?
C You can't tell?

Question 10

What is your opinion about negotiating? Is it

A Finding the most acceptable compromise?
B Making a decision with another person that meets as many of that person's and as many of your interests as possible?
C Give and take?
D A fair and equal transaction?

That's the end of the quiz. Now let's have a look at the answers and, equally important, the thoughts behind them.

While selling a vintage car or travelling across the desert may not appear over-relevant to your selling situation, there are lessons to be learnt from all these questions that will, I'm sure, be invaluable to us in our sales and negotiating careers.

Answers

			Score
1.	The vintage car, advertised at £30,000		
	A	Wait until the advert: you might lose the sale to this buyer altogether.	–20
	B	Haggle: this is the correct thing to do. We must always, always haggle, however good the first offer appears to be.	+30
	C	Take the £32,000: never, ever, accept the first offer on anything.	–20
2.	The speedboat, £11,000. You can raise £9,500		
	A	Phone your spouse: it may appear to be a bargain, but how do you *know* it is?	–20
	B	'An offer you can't refuse': it is definitely an offer you *can* refuse.	–30
	C	An awful position: whenever anybody accepts your first offer you must be thinking you could have started with a lower figure and bought the product at a cheaper price.	+30
3.	Landlord, rent increase of 30 per cent		
	A	Write immediately detailing problems: this is a great way to start any negotiation, by opening at a point well below the current situation.	+30
	B	Ask for a rent reduction: this would make a strong opening, but is better if used in conjunction with A.	+20
	C	Offer 15 per cent: the problem with offering 15 per cent at this point is you are likely to end up with a 'splitting the difference' situation.	–20
	D	Suggest rent tribunal: if you go to the rent tribunal, you've completely removed your chance of vetoing the decision.	–30
4.	Van breaks down, a local businessman offers his		
	A	Solicitors' contract: unfortunately, the factors in the question show you don't have time to go to your solicitors to draw up a contract.	0

B Sign as requested: this is an extremely risky thing to do both for you and for your business colleague. −20

C Receipt isn't necessary: this is not just risky, it's downright dangerous. −30

D Ask for more information: we need to ask lots of 'if' and 'what if' questions. For example, 'What if someone runs into the van?' 'What if it's stolen?' 'If there is a problem with the van, whose insurance is going to cover it?' +20

5. Widget buyer at airport

A Quote high price: this is a reasonable move. You have not fallen for his power-play tactics, but it's still not the best move you could make. +10

B You'll cut price if given an order: if the buyer has made you concede such a large amount at this first, five-minute meeting, what's likely to be the situation in a major meeting? −30

C Quote lowest possible price: his power-play tactics have definitely worked. −80

D Give him your best wishes for his trip: the correct move. At this point in the negotiation you do not know how badly he needs your product. Give him all your best wishes for his trip and tell him you'll arrange to meet with his staff to find out how you can best service his need. It may well be they have a major problem and need you more than you need them. +60

6. Negotiating with large company. You've given price, he says: 'You'll have to do better than that'

A Ask the difference between your price and other prices: I'm sure you've found, as I've found, that some buyers don't always tell you all the truth. There is a possibility you'll get bluffed on the differences. −20

B You'll cut price for order: at this stage you have no idea exactly what the other quotations are, and there is a chance the buyer will tell you. However much you offer to cut the price, it simply isn't enough. −30

C Ask what he likes about your proposal: the correct thing to do. If you can find out the hot buttons from your proposal, you can concentrate on those. Price is not the only factor in any buying or selling situation. +20

D See the other offers: this is a good move, if you actually believe there are other offers, but if there aren't this can create an embarrassing or difficult situation. 0

E Tentatively suggest he accepts other offers: certainly a strong move, but if he is bluffing, you may have blown the negotiation. +10

7. Updating your computer: how much?

A 20 per cent: we seldom get more than we expect to get. +30

B 15 per cent: not too bad, but let's up our expectations. +20

C None: what can I say? –30

D 5 per cent: I realise you were probably trying to be realistic, but there are certainly excellent discounts available from most manufacturers given sufficient time and planning on negotiation. +10

8. Toy washing-machine, nursery matron; £1,800 retail, offer of £1,600

A Deal not possible: certainly a strong stance but perhaps better used after C. +10

B Accept offer: the matron has used a technique on you called the 'Mother Hubbard' or, in other words, 'the cupboard is bare'. You will find, I'm sure, that many customers use this idea; however, they usually say, 'We've used our budget for this year' or some similar expression. –25

C Benefits of machine costing £1,575: this is the correct move. +15

9. Man selling water in desert; price one camel. Who has power?

A The man with the camels. –20

B The man with the water. –20

C You can't tell: there is insufficient information to tell who has the power. For example, the man with the camels may have a shotgun. The man with the water may have a million camels and not need any more. There simply isn't enough information to make a decision. +20

10. What is your opinion about negotiating?

A Acceptable compromise: it will all depend on to whom it's most acceptable. If we're going to end up 'splitting the difference', that is not negotiation. 0

B Meeting of mutual interests: the correct answer. You are the best judge of your interests and the other party is the best judge of their interests. +20

C Give and take: negotiation is definitely not about give and take, particularly if you give more than you take. –10

D Fair and equal transaction: negotiations are usually fair but seldom equal. –20

The steps to success

Step 1

As we have discussed, we must listen carefully – we must listen *actively* and try to understand what it is the buyer wants as an end result of the negotiation. We may well be prepared to give something quite easily that the buyer wants: don't jump in and give it away. Listen for the end results.

Step 2

Never concede, trade. For example: 'Will you place the order now if I arrange for delivery on Friday?' By using that powerful word 'IF' you haven't said you will arrange for delivery on Friday, you've just said that 'if' you do, will the buyer place the order?

So often in negotiations people concede a point without taking something in return. This comes back to our point about give and take. Could it be that a customer wants to pay a particular price for your goods and, if you're prepared to concede that price, *you* want a contract for the next *five* years? Always, always trade.

Step 3

Let go of the negotiations emotionally before you actually start the process. I once saw this written as: 'Take the ego out of n**EGO**tiation.'

It's so much easier when we are buying products for other people rather than buying them for ourselves. You'll have been in this situation and know that you're quite prepared to walk away from the situation because it doesn't hurt emotionally. If we are able to maintain that attitude while buying or selling, we can be firmer in our negotiating stance.

Step 4

We must use this idea of hurt and rescue or, in other words, we must frighten people with our first offer. If we are buying an item priced at £100 and we offer £90 to start with, the likelihood is we'll end at £95. If, on the other hand, we offer £50 to start with there is a greater chance of ending at £60 or £70.

I'm reminded of the story of the girl on the train who (and this was many years ago) got into a carriage where there was no corridor. There was a man sitting opposite her. Looking at this particularly attractive girl, he took out his wallet and started counting £50 notes on to the table between them.

'If I give you £10,000, would you go out to dinner with me tonight?' said the man.

The girl thought about the implications of the offer for a minute and then said: 'Yes, for £10,000 I will.'

The man collected the money from the table and put it back into his inside pocket. He looked at the girl, smiled and said: 'Would you go to dinner with me for £1?'

The girl immediately responded: 'No! What sort of a girl do you think I am?'

The man replied: 'I think we know what sort of girl you are. We just have to establish the right price!'

If we are able, over the course of our commercial and social lives, to increase the number of times we negotiate, our skills will increase. I do believe that negotiation in your private life when buying, be it for clothes, houses, cars or even holidays, will assist you in your selling role. Being able to see the picture from the buyer's point of view is one of the key steps in planning your negotiation tactics.

Over the years I've bought items priced at £65 for only £5, items priced at £11 for only £1 and, naturally, the negotiations didn't start off at 10 per cent off the retail price.

What you often find will happen is that, when you make a ridiculous first offer, with a smile on your face, the response will be 'What! But it's made of . . .' The other party will give you a list of *features,* not benefits, of the product. Your response is simple: 'Yes, I know, that's why I want to buy it.'

Make absolutely certain that, while you are negotiating, if the other party moves towards you on price, you don't move. This does *not* mean you have to move just because they do. Stick firm, stand your ground and you will be amazed at how cheaply you can get most of the items you buy during the course of your commercial and social life.

Step 5

The following are a few ideas you'll be able to use when buying. On a recent seminar I ran for a multinational company, we had a similar discussion about negotiation. Within one week one of the young men on the course had written to me saying that, in the first few days after the course, he had saved himself by simple negotiation over £300. Sometimes we just have to ask for a discount to get it.

You will recall our discussion about the technique of 'Did you do Latin?' when we were talking about what we say. You can use this idea when negotiating in shops. Walking into the shop, you smile pleasantly at the staff or manager and ask to see the item in which you are interested. As you are walking away from the counter to where the item is situated, you say casually: 'Before I look at the item, I must just tell you I never, ever pay retail. That's OK, isn't it?'

Invariably people will respond 'Yes' and you've set up the situation ready to negotiate the price for when you have decided on the product. They've already agreed you never pay retail. Use this idea – it certainly works.

I once went into a dress shop in Birmingham with my wife. We'd been to the dress shop before and I knew that price was negotiable. As we walked into the shop the lady who owned it was there. I explained we had come to look at a dress or dresses and used my usual line: 'You remember, as I was here before, that I never pay retail for anything. That's OK isn't it?' (I'd anticipated getting a 15–20-per-cent discount.)

The lady's response astounded me. She replied with a lop-sided smile: 'I suppose you're one of those people who always want 30 per cent off everything aren't you?'

What was my response? I didn't say 'Yes'. I said, 'No, I was looking for at least 50 per cent.' If you remember back to our quiz, we never,

ever accept the first offer. We ended at 35 per cent and I was well pleased with the purchase, as was my wife.

The second method you can use in getting discounts is as follows. Having decided on your purchase, and gone to the counter to pay, you say to the person behind the counter, again always with a smile: 'Tell me, do you have the authority to give discounts?' What are the possible answers?

1. *Yes.* Instantly you know discounts are available and it is up to you to negotiate the best deal possible.
2. *No.* In this case, again in a soft voice with a smile, you would simply say, 'Oh? Who does?' The response will usually be the manager or the assistant manager or whoever. Ask to speak to them. When the manager appears, you again smile and say in a soft voice, 'I understand from your assistant that *you* have the authority to give discounts. Is that right?' This will guarantee a 'Yes' reply and, again, it will be up to you to negotiate the best deal possible.

I was once in a major store in Birmingham, making a purchase of several hundred pounds. When I was at the counter, a very pleasant lady was prepared to ring up the sale on her till but, before she did, I said to her: 'Tell me, do you have the authority to give discounts?'

'No', was her reply.

'Who does?'

'Oh, it's the floor manager.'

'Please may I see him?'

Off she went to get him and over he strode. He was obviously an ex-military man by his bearing, and I'm sure you can imagine the situation.

'Your sales assistant tells me *you* have the authority to give discounts. Is that right?' I asked.

Standing even straighter than before and pushing out his chest, he proudly told me 'Yes'. Negotiation was fairly straightforward from that point onward.

You will be able to use the following if you are dealing with intermediaries, estate agents or brokers. It's based on the same idea as 'do you have the authority?'

Some years ago I was buying a flat for my mother and, as I wasn't buying it for my own use, I was able to be particularly tough in the negotiations. The estate agent concerned in the sale knew I was interested in buying and phoned me regularly. Where possible I avoided his calls and really pressured the situation.

Finally agreeing to meet him at the property concerned one

morning, I opened with the line: 'I know I've been difficult to get hold of, but I only like to deal with the principals in any negotiation.'

His response was a simple 'Why?'

I responded with: 'I will only ever deal with someone who has the authority to negotiate the price.'

His response: 'But I *can* negotiate the price!'

You can imagine the situation from there on.

Step 6

Planning: here we use our old friend, the 'Six Ps Principle', which stands for 'Proper Planning Prevents Particularly Poor Performance'.

The more time we spend on planning, the less time we normally need to spend on the negotiation itself. The areas of planning I believe we should look at are as follows:

1. We need to do research into the other party. If we are in a selling situation, what is the position of the buyer's company's finances? Have we previously sold to this company and are there members of your company who can advise as to the buyer's negotiation tactics?

   Are we able to speak to the buyer's staff? Do we know the buyer's thoughts on status? Have our previous conversations uncovered the hot buttons? Find out as much as possible.
2. Define your goals: decide before you enter the negotiation what your best outcome will be, what a realistic outcome will be and what your 'worst take' position is.
3. Know the competition. Any of us involved in the selling business should be aware of the terms of business of our major competitors. Is it that other companies can offer something we can't? If this is the case, we need to have good, well-thought-out reasons to counter these points.
4. Take to the negotiation all the necessary paperwork to prove any points you might make.
5. Find out who else will be involved in the negotiation. Did you think you would be dealing with just one person and then, at crunch time, three others came into the room?

   If this ever happens to you, and it's happened to me, then ask questions to find out who has the authority to buy. This is not to say that you will concentrate only on that person, because the others may be decision influencers. However, at least you'll know who has to say 'Yes'.
6. Spend time looking at the negotiation, during your planning stage, from the buyer's point of view. I once saw this written as

follows: 'You can't get into somebody else's shoes until you take off your own.' Write down the questions you would ask if you were the buyer and, of course, make sure you can answer all those possible questions.

7. Calculate the real cost of any concessions you may be preparing to make. A simple discount of 2½ per cent may appear very small. However, if your margin is only 10 per cent, you just gave away 25 per cent of your margin.
8. Plan to keep notes during the course of the negotiation so you can summarise regularly. If you have decided to give way on a number of points, you will need to keep telling the buyer you've given way.

Price

Before we finish the steps in negotiation, let's look at the area of price. As we all know, 'price' is only one factor in the negotiation. However, it can often be a major stumbling block while we are still inexperienced.

Many years ago one of my colleagues went on a sales-training course and came back with this idea, which we've used ever since. It goes as follows. The presenter asked Richard, one of the delegates, to leave the room for a few moments. He then asked another of the delegates, Tim, to join him at the front, and said: 'Tim, what I want us to do now is to have a short role-play session on negotiation. Here is the situation. I am a second-hand car salesman and you have come into my garage. In front of us is a white Ford XR3i priced at £5,000.

'*You have decided to buy it.* This is a most important point. You have decided to buy it and we're now going to negotiate the price.

'We're going to have fun with this and add in all sorts of things we probably wouldn't add in in real life. It's only to make a point.

'I'm going to start off by closing you on the sale and you will resist the close, Tim. Then we'll negotiate the price.

'Remember the golden rule of negotiation: frighten them with your first offer. OK, Tim, off we go.'

Presenter (as salesman); 'Well, Tim, you've obviously fallen in love with the car. Would delivery next Tuesday be soon enough?' (The enough close.)

'Well, I don't know about that, Peter. I'm not very happy with the price.'

'How much would you like to pay me for it?'

'I'll pay you £2,000.'

'£2,000! What! But it's an Escort XR3i and it's got metallic paint work and a super-charged engine and the seats are black. Surely you can pay more than £2,000?' (Note only features being described, not benefits.)

'Well, perhaps I might squeeze myself to £2,500.'

'Look, Tim, I'll tell you what I'll do. I'll put some road tax into the deal, and I could probably do the deal for £4,721.'

'No, no, no. I can't afford anything like that. I might manage £3,000.'

'I'm sorry, Tim, I just can't sell you this car for £3,000. However, if I was able to bring my price down to £4,600, what would I need to add in to the deal for you to want to buy it?'

'Well, I'd need alloy wheels and a new stereo and one year's road tax.'

'So, if I add in alloy wheels, one year's road tax and a new stereo and the price is £4,601.50, will you buy it?'

'Um, I'm not sure. I'm really concerned about servicing.'

'Tell me, Tim, what would you like on servicing?'

'Well, I'll definitely need the car serviced before I buy it and really I'd like the next service thrown in as well. Does that *sound* OK?'

'Tim, I *hear* what you say. If I was able to put a new radio in, put alloy wheels on, put a year's road tax in, service the car before you have it and arrange for the next service to be free, will you give me £4,175?'

'Peter, I can't quite manage that, but I'll give you £3,800.'

'Tim, I can't take £3,800 but I will take £3,970 if we can leave out that second service. Is that a deal?'

'OK, Peter, that's a deal!'

As you will realise this was only a role-play situation and, in reality, the price isn't likely to get to that stage. I've just tried to add in a number of variables to make the negotiation interesting.

Tim was asked if he was happy with the deal, and he said he was. He felt he'd struck a good bargain, buying a £5,000 car for £3,970. Richard, who was sent out earlier, was asked to come back in.

'Richard, will you join me at the front? We're going to have a role play on negotiation. We're just going to have a bit of fun. Let me explain the situation. I am a second-hand car salesman and you have come into my garage. In front of us is a white Ford XR3i priced at £5,000.

'*You have decided to buy it.* This is a most important point. You have decided to buy it and we're now going to negotiate the price.

'We're going to have fun with this and add in all sorts of things we probably wouldn't add in in real life. It's only to make a point.

'I'm going to start off by closing you on the sale and you will resist the close, Richard. Then we'll negotiate the price.

'Remember the golden rule of negotiation: frighten them with your first offer. OK, Richard, off we go.'

Presenter (as salesman): 'Well, Richard, you've obviously fallen in love with the car. Would delivery next Tuesday be soon enough?'

'Well, I do like the car, Peter, but I'm not too happy with the price. I'll give you £2,500 for it.'

The presenter then thrust out his hand, Richard shook it and the presenter said: 'It's yours, thank you, sit down.'

Here is a strange situation. Richard is extremely *unhappy* and yet he's bought a car for £2,500. Tim, on the other hand, is extremely *happy* but he's paid £3,970.

How is it that Tim has paid more and is happy, and Richard has paid less and is unhappy? The reason is really quite simple, isn't it? Sometimes it isn't the price that matters but how we actually get to the price. Let's make sure our negotiations allow buyers to score points so they can satisfy their egos. It may well be that what the buyer wants we're prepared to give; however, we wouldn't just give it away, we would always trade it.

Moving on in our discussion about price, people often say to us that our price is too high. (If people don't say your price is too high, could it be too low?) But in reality they may mean something totally different. Here are my thoughts:

1. You've surprised me. I thought it would probably be cheaper than that.
2. I'm employed to reduce the price, or get discounts.
3. I have a quote from another company that appears to be cheaper. (Do you find that customers don't always compare apples with apples and, sometimes, when they say they have a cheaper price, it's really not for the same specification?)
4. It's over my personal buying limit. (Often the customers who have confirmed to you at the start of a negotiation or selling situation that they are the people who make the decision, yet when all the factors of the sale are added up, the price is over their limit. They don't like to admit that and may well try to negotiate the price until it is within their own personal buying limits.)
5. It's outside the budget.
6. We've got a cash-flow problem.

All those ideas could be reasons why a potential customer is telling you your product or service is too expensive, and the only way we will uncover the real reason is by asking questions. Not only questions at this point in the conversation but also, of course, questions throughout the sale. We must also make careful notes of the information we obtain.

The point about cash-flow problem or 'There's no money left' can be used in negotiations of your own. I read in that excellent book by Gavin Kennedy, *Everything is Negotiable,* a technique regarding this, and I used it as follows. In one of my companies we needed a new typist's chair. My secretary, knowing my penchant for buying things at the right price, suggested we phone our usual office-equipment supplier and buy a chair priced £65. There were two chairs shown in the catalogue, one at £85 and one at £65. With Kennedy's ideas in mind, I said I would deal with the situation.

I telephoned the supplier and said: 'Malcolm, I have some great news. I want to place an order.'

'That's good,' he said, 'What do you want?'

'I want a typist's chair. Here's the number out of your catalogue. The price is £85. Do you have one in stock?'

'Yes, we do.'

'When could I have delivery, please?'

'I'll have it delivered tomorrow.'

'That's great, Malcolm, thanks very much indeed. But, just one thing before you go. We have no money at the moment . . .'

Malcolm said: 'How do you mean?'

'Well, we have no money for chairs at the moment. I'd like to have the chair but I'd like to pay nothing at all for it. That'll be OK, won't it?'

Malcolm stuttered and stammered and um'ed and ah'ed and finally said: 'Yes, that'll be fine.'

'Thanks, Malcolm, goodbye.'

I simply could not believe how that worked. It was straight out of the book, exactly to the script and saved me £85. I know it seems incredible, but try it: what's the worst that can happen?

My final idea on price, before we move on to the final steps, is as follows. When I was running Compass Leasing plc in Birmingham, we were a leasing brokerage company and would therefore arrange leases between our customer's customer, the end user of the goods, and a finance house. Because we were a broker we were naturally more expensive than if the customer was able to deal directly with the finance house. However, we did have something else to offer. We were able to offer speed and service and, perhaps more importantly, we were fun to deal with.

We made it fun for the customers. Business was done with a smile. We cared about the service we were giving, we made sure the customer got the product when it was needed by arranging the finance as quickly as possible. And yet we were more expensive. Price isn't everything: let's not get hung up on price. It's only one factor in any negotiation.

More steps to success

Step 7

If you decide to make a move, make it seem large; for example, if you're going to give 2½-per-cent discount on an order for £100,000, the discount is £2,500. Let's not talk about 2½ per cent, let's talk about £2,500.

Step 8

If the buyer concedes a point we need to minimise it. That's not to say we criticise it, but we need to find a way to explain politely to the buyer that the buyer's concession is really not worth a great deal.

Step 9

When you give the price, sandwich it between two benefits. State a benefit, give the price, state another benefit; and then ask for the order.

Step 10

Never assume – always, always, actively listen.

Complaints

Making complaints and receiving complaints is an ideal opportunity to practise our negotiation skills and there is a simple formula to use.

When most people take a product back to a business or shop in order to complain, they basically say they're not very happy about the situation and they go on to state the reason. This can often be done in an aggressive and embarrassing way. The system I use, which I learnt some years ago, is as follows:

1. Simply state, 'I'm not happy.'
2. Then say, 'And the reason I'm not happy is . . .' and *calmly* explain the problem.
3. Then say, 'However, this is what will make me happy . . .' and go on to explain exactly what will resolve the situation.

By giving the other party a 'way out' of the problem, provided that way out is reasonable, you will often find they will take your suggestion. No one has become entrenched in a particular position. No one is feeling defensive or annoyed. It is a simple and effective way to resolve complaints.

For example, let's assume you have checked into a hotel. You have gone to your room and you're not happy with the room for some reason. You would go back to reception and say: 'I'm not happy, and the reason I am not happy is that the room is (whatever is wrong). However, what will make me happy is if you move me to a different room and give me a bottle of wine with my dinner. That's OK isn't it?' This works: try it.

When we are receiving complaints we use the same idea. We say to our customers: 'I understand you're not happy, and the reason you're not happy is . . .' Here we clearly reflect the exact words used by our customers so they know we are actively listening: 'Tell me, Mr Customer, what would make you happy?'

The customer will then go on to explain what will make him or her happy and, provided it is a reasonable request and you're happy to provide what the customer wants, you respond with: 'So, Mr Customer, if I . . . then you will be happy, is that right?'

The customer responds with 'Yes' and you simply say: 'I'll go and make it happen.'

Review plan

Name ______________________________

Topic ______________________ **Date** __________

Notes ______________________________

Action	Target date	Completion date
1.		
2.		
3.		
4.		
5.		
6.		

CHAPTER 12

Goal setting

The ability to set goals and to work an effective action plan towards those goals is another of the 'must haves' for success.

In 1953 a study was done at Harvard University where the class of that year was set a test. One of the purposes of that test was to find out if the participants had set written goals. It was found that only *3 per cent* had set goals.

Twenty years later, yes, 20 years later, the same people were asked to fill in another questionnaire. The information the researchers were looking for in particular was the success of the students and their financial position: their worth in monetary terms. (However, we're all aware that financial worth is only one measure of success.) The 3 per cent, it was found, were worth more financially than the 97 per cent put together. Research says that all major achievers in all fields set goals.

Everyone says that setting goals is important. Every personal-development training or sales-training manual, seminar or tape says that goal setting is important. If that is the case, why is it that people do not set goals?

On page 128 you will see a list of 11 reasons why people don't set goals, and I'd like you to put a tick against *your* reasons: the reasons you don't set goals or you don't have up-to-date written goals – and that word *written* is most important. If they're not written down then they're only dreams and, at this stage, while dreams can come true, it is more likely that a properly written goal with an action plan to achieve that goal will succeed.

Let me ask another question. Do you really want to get something out of your life? Another question: imagine I had a magic wand. I came round and tapped you on the shoulder with it so you could have one wish. Yes, just one wish (that wish can't be to have more wishes, by the way). What would you wish for in your life? Could it be that there is already someone in the world living your dream, that they've set that goal and taken the actions to achieve it?

On an audiotape presentation by Zig Ziglar, that well-known American trainer, I heard him put it this way:

Why I have not set written goals, or why I have not updated my goals

	Tick box
1. Fear of failure	
2. Don't know how to set goals	
3. Too impatient	
4. Major goals seem unattainable	
5. Fear of rejection	
6. Do not make the time	
7. Self-limiting beliefs	
8. Don't realise the importance of goals	
9. Fear of criticism	
10. No ambition	
11. Other reasons	

Question: 'What is three times three?'
Answer: 'Nine.'
Question: 'What is 3,742 × 1,964?'

We all know it's difficult to work out the second answer in our heads. However, having the formula based on three times three, we could come up with the answer – given time.

Goal setting is exactly like that. If we have a simple formula we can follow, then actually setting out goals, while time consuming, will be possible.

The ideas I'm about to share with you are a simple formula to enable you to set your goals. Imagine the following situation. Some prisoners have escaped. What invariably happens within three days of their escape? Yes, they get recaptured and put back into prison.

This is simply because they have planned to *become* free, not to *be* free. We therefore need to be careful when we're setting our own goals that we plan what's going to happen past the point of having achieved the goal.

So often people achieve goals in life only to have a feeling of anti-climax. You'll know the situation, someone works extremely hard to move from being a member of the salesforce to being the sales manager. When they get to be sales manager, they've made it! But they then stop doing the things that got them the promotion in the first place. We must plan to *be* not just to *become*.

Write down the goals you would like to have achieved in five years' time. List them as quickly as possible because your brain works well when it works quickly, and don't be restricted to the obvious – look at all these areas:

1. Travel
2. Career
3. Cars
4. Home
5. Health
6. Mind (more learning)
7. Finances
8. Friendships
9. Children and family
10. Community service
11. Recreation and leisure

. . . and any others you can think of.

In five years' time I would like to have achieved:

____

____

____

What goals would you like to have achieved in one year?

The goals I would like to achieve in one year are:

____

____

____

What goals would you like to have achieved in three months' time?

The goals I would like to have achieved in three months are:

____

____

____

Now what we do is go back to each of those lists and prioritise them. The easiest way to put them in order is to mark them A, B and C.

A: For the things you'd really love to have achieved.
B: For the things it would be nice to achieve.
C: For, well, if you had time you probably would.

Do exactly the same with your one-year goals and your three-month goals. Now let's look at those and make sure they are balanced.

The things you're going to achieve in three months are going to lead you to the things you want to achieve in one year, which in turn will lead you to the things you want to achieve in five years.

Now what we need to do is to go back to our five-year, one-year and three-month goals and cross out everything except the As. I'm sure you will find some of the Bs relate to the As anyway, and if you could only mark them B and C at this stage there is little point keeping them on our list.

The next thing to do is to write out each of those A goals on a separate sheet of paper, making sure they follow the 'Peter Principle':

P precise
E exciting
T truthful
E effective action
R recordable

Let me expand on this. By precise I mean we have to be very, very, precise, and very, very, specific with the goal. There is little point saying, 'I want to be slim.' There's no way you will know if you've ever achieved it. We need to put on a time or an amount or a date. Make that goal as precise as possible.

Second, we need to make sure our goals are exciting. If the goal does not excite us there is no motivation to achieve it.

Third, we need to make sure our goal is truthful. There seems little point to me setting a goal to fly by your own power to the moon during the next month. It just will not happen. Make sure your goals are balanced between exciting and truthful.

Fourth, our goals need to involve us in taking effective action because, if we're relying on someone else to take actions to achieve our goals, it's unlikely they will be attained. I discuss later how to work out the effective actions.

Finally, our goals need to be recordable. If we don't have two record systems (one that clearly tells us when we have achieved the goal and one that records our progress along the way), we won't know if we're on the right track and we won't know when we arrive.

You can imagine the situation where you were playing golf and didn't have a score card, how would you know who had won? If you'd been to a football match and, when you arrived home, someone said to you: 'What was the match like?' and you went on with a 90-minute explanation of what actually happened. 'Well, they put the ball in the middle of the field and somebody kicked it forward and . . .' No, it's far easier to be able to say, 'They won, three, two.' The score card is essential in so many areas of our lives.

A word of warning. Setting goals will take time. A great deal of time, but it will be worth every minute you ever spend. Decide now to take the time to set goals for all the areas of your life. After all, *if you don't know where you're going . . . all the roads lead there.*

Our next job, and this really will give us the main motivation to achieve our goals, is to answer one simple question about each of those goals – and answer it in *writing* on that sheet. The question is: WHY?

Why do you want to achieve this goal? Use the major motivators of pain and pleasure to find out the reasons why you really *must* achieve this goal.

If you don't know why you want to do it – that is, if you're not avoiding pain or gaining pleasure – there is probably little chance you will ever have the success you believe you want. Take the time to do that now.

Our brains are complex pieces of equipment and all the books I've read about how the brain works discuss the idea of the 'reticular activation system'. This is like a filter in your head, which stops you consciously receiving information. You can imagine if, going through the day, you were consciously aware of every single thing that was happening about you, every noise, every feeling, every sight – our senses would be overwhelmed with information. The reticular activation system blocks out, filters out certain things it believes your brain doesn't consciously need.

For example, what is your left foot doing now? Until I asked that question you were probably totally unaware of what it was doing in a conscious way; now that it's been mentioned you are consciously aware. Well, how can this help us?

It can be of tremendous benefit to us with goal setting. The way we open that filter, the way we open that gate to let information into our minds regarding our wishes, desires and goals is to say simply 'I am . . .'. For example: 'I am 13 st 7 lbs and the date is the 5th of April 2001.' Saying 'I am' sets up the pressure within you to take the actions to achieve the goals. Your brain seems to be saying, 'either stop saying

I am 13 st 7 lb or do something about it!' I'm sure you'll be aware of this situation and have had this happen to you.

You've decided to buy a new car. You've decided on the colour and the model and suddenly you see that same car everywhere. Is it the fact that everyone has suddenly decided to buy the same car? No, it's simply the fact that you are now aware, you've opened that gate, you've removed the filter.

Perhaps you've decided to buy a TV and you look in your evening paper. Suddenly there's hundreds of TV advertisements. How did everybody know to place their advert on the night you were looking? Of course they didn't: those ads were always there, you just didn't see them. Has that happened to you?

Now we know our goals for three months, one year and five years, and we know why we want to achieve them and we've written them in such a way as to make them precise, excitable, truthful, involves us in effective action and are recordable, we need to work out the actions we must take to achieve our goals.

Let's have another quiz at this stage. You are a tennis-tournament organiser and you have been asked to organise a singles knockout tennis tournament. Some 257 people apply to play. You decide they can all play.

The question is: how many matches altogether will you need to arrange? Not how many in each round, but how many altogether? Take a few moments and try to work that out. Half will play half in the first round, and then half will go through, etc., to the final. The answer is 256 matches, and we calculate it as follows.

At the end of the day there will be only one winner who holds the cup aloft, and therefore there must be 256 losers. As it's a singles knockout competition, everybody only loses once. How many matches will there be to get 256 losers? Answer: 256 matches.

The relevance of this question to goal setting is as follows. The simple way to work out the route to the final was to know the end result. If we take but a few moments with each of our goals to visualise ourselves as though we had already achieved the goals, the road or actions we need to take will be obvious.

For my own goal-setting activities I regularly use the idea of 'The Yesterday's Road Philosophy', but I do it in a surprisingly negative way. In my mind I go forward to the point when I would like to have achieved the goal. I then imagine, albeit only briefly, that I have *not* achieved the goal and I say to myself: 'If only I'd . . . I would have achieved the goal.' I then work out what those dots are.

Most of us know most of the actions we need to take to achieve our goals, and we don't have a plan of action we can follow. Using this

Yesterday's Road Philosophy of 'If only I'd . . .' can be extremely effective.

When I was running Compass Leasing plc and we'd sold out to a public company, halfway through the earnout year we lost a major client, through no fault of our own, but it looked as though we wouldn't hit the projected figures. I gathered my fellow directors together and said the following: 'Imagine now that it's six months in the future. It's the 31st of March and we haven't hit the figures. Please answer this question for me. If only I'd . . . we *would* have hit the figures. What are those dots?'

Within about half an hour the directors came up with a list of actions they knew they should have taken for us to hit the figures. Within half a day I had an action plan using their ideas and my ideas for the next six months. We hit the figures. Use this idea of 'If only I'd . . .' It really can work extremely well for you.

You now need to take some time to work out the actions you know you must take to achieve those goals. Those are the A goals for your three-month, one-year and five-year sheets.

While doing this, ensure your goals are balanced. For example, if you've decided you want to be the top salesperson in your company and you want to be a scratch golfer (though currently playing off an 18 handicap), it is unlikely you'll achieve both. Decide which is more important and prepare your action plans accordingly.

We now have our written goals in place for three months, one year and five years, and we must set up a record system to make sure we stay on track. The first thing to do is to put a forward date in your diary for the date on which the goal will have been achieved. The second is to put in 'stops' along the way where you can measure your progress towards the goal. This can be a sheet in the back of your diary with a list of dates and the progress you should have made by a particular date, or you can use the diary pages themselves if it's a short-term goal.

Here are three further ideas that will assist you to stay on track.

Affirmations

If you use the type of diary that is a small ring-binder you can prepare for yourself on card, with appropriately punched holes, an affirmation sheet regarding your goals. By affirmations I mean that your goals are written down, they're positive, they're in the present tense and they're illogical.

Positive

By positive I mean you mustn't include any negative words, such as not, unless, etc., because your brain simply cannot cope with them. Let me explain: the brain works in pictures. Try to write a picture for 'not'. It's impossible. Another example: don't think of a dog chasing a cat. You have to think of it in order to be able *not* to think of it.

Present tense

We need to write our affirmations in the present tense using the idea of 'I am' to open the reticular activation gate or filter. If we set our goals saying, 'I will be' or 'I want to be', every time we say them we haven't achieved them and the 'I will . . .' means it will always be tomorrow. Setting them in the present tense by using 'I am' or 'I have', we set up the appropriate pressures.

Illogical

By illogical I mean, if you set a goal to achieve something you've already achieved, there is no pressure on you. If you set goals to achieve those things you have not yet achieved but you're still saying they *have* happened, you will again set up the pressure on your mind to motivate you to take the appropriate actions.

Audio tape

Prepare an audio-tape for yourself, a simple production on your home tape-recorder where you read out your own goals, using the ideas of positive, present and illogical. This can be five or ten minutes long at best, and it doesn't need any elaborate production with introduction, music or sound effects – just your own voice, reading out your goals using the system I have described.

This makes it extremely easy, on a daily basis, to plan your actions for the day because you can hear your goals at the push of a button. If you're not taking actions each day towards your goals, are you going to achieve them? Unlikely.

Visualisation

My suggestion is you take a quiet moment on your own to sit and to visualise yourself clearly in a position where the goal has already been achieved. All the books I've read, all the tapes I've listened to, all my experiences indicate that visualisation, for some strange reason, makes things happen!

Goal record sheet

Goal ____

Why ____

Date	Action to have been taken	Yes	No

Goal sheet

My goal is

____

____

____

(NB Precise/Exciting/Truthful/Effective action/Recordable)

Why? (Pain/Pleasure)

____

____

____

____

____

Rewards
When I achieve my goal I will reward myself by

____

____

____

____

As I reach each stage along the road to my goal I will reward myself by

____

____

____

The steps to success

Step 1

Decide to set goals.

Step 2

Set goals for five years, one year and three months.

Step 3

Prioritise.

Step 4

Cross out the Bs and Cs and write the As on a separate sheet.

Step 5

Ensure they follow the Peter Principle.

Step 6

Write a powerful 'Why' statement using pain and pleasure to motivate you into action.

Step 7

Use the Yesterday's Road Philosophy or the idea of the tennis matches to decide on the actions you must take.

Step 8

Set up your record systems.

Step 9

Prepare your affirmations sheet and audio-tape, and take time to visualise your goals having been achieved. This is essential for your success.

Step 10

Use the mirror theory we discussed in positive attitudes to self-manage your actions and emotions.

Step 11

If you're going to share your goals with anyone, only *ever* share them with positive and supportive people who will help you to achieve. As a general rule it is better not to share them with anyone.

Further thoughts on goal setting

Make sure you are prepared to be changeable with your goals. As Maxwell Maltz said in his excellent book, *Psychocybernetics*: 'If you have launched a torpedo towards an enemy ship, it's likely the ship will move.' By noting the movements, the feedback, you can change the path of the torpedo to ensure it does hit its goal. Phrased differently, failure isn't falling down: failure is not getting up again.

For most of us our goals do change and we need to make sure we've not cast them in stone by telling the world about them so we can make the appropriate changes and stay on the new track.

When you spend time setting your social and home-life goals, my suggestion is you do them on your own and not with your spouse. Ask your spouse to do them separately and then compare notes. In that way you get a more accurate assessment of everyone's real desires.

If you do not find time in your life to prepare the action plans and take the actions you have decided on from any of the topics in this book, then I urge you, in the strongest possible terms, to take the time to set your goals. It's always said that the people who don't set goals end up working for the people who do.

Remember, what you set is what you get. If you set nothing, you get nothing. If you set everything . . . you get everything.

CHAPTER 13

Creative action

Well, that goal-setting topic was fairly heavy stuff, wasn't it? Let's move on to a lighter area and talk about how we can be more creative: more creative in our business life, in our social life, in fact, in all areas of our lives.

Tests

Test 1

As a mark out of 100, how creative are you?

Test 2

(a) Have you ever been in a traffic jam and then found your way round it so you arrived at your destination on time?
(b) Have you ever decorated a room or chosen the carpets and curtains?
(c) Did you decide what to wear today?
(d) Have you ever painted a picture in your life?
(e) Have you ever taken a photograph and decided where you wanted the people to stand, or decided on the result you were looking for?
(f) Have you ever helped customers by explaining how the benefits will create results for them?
(g) Have you ever designed a letterhead, a form or paperwork of any description?
(h) Have you ever planned a route to somewhere?
(i) Have you ever planned a party or a social gathering?
(j) Are you aware that positive expectation can, almost instantly increase our skill levels in a variety of areas?

Test 3

Having looked at your answers to the previous ten questions, mark yourself again out of 100. How creative are you?

If we believe we are creative we increase our chances of being creative.

One of the keys to creativity is having a good memory. A long time ago I took a memory course that used a memory-hook system: if you haven't taken a memory course I suggest you do.

We have discussed the five keys to memory, namely: primacy, immediacy, linking, unusual things and reviews. Use all these areas to increase your memory. For example, when you review your personal notes from the 'key word' and 'picture notes' you've taken from this book, do so on a regular basis to move the information into your long-term memory.

Let's take a moment to find out how creative we really can be. This is called the 'paper-clip test'. I'd like you to write down all the uses for a paper-clip or paper-clips that you can think of. You can be as outrageous as you like, but you have only two minutes to do it – starting now.

One seminar group came up with 60 ideas to use a paper-clip. They included a brooch, a nail cleaner, a hook, a repair to a side arm on a pair of glasses, a fuse, a shoelace, a sundial, a pen, a ring, a key, a watch strap, a coat-hanger and a vast variety of other ideas.

Research says that, if we are able to come up with just four items in two minutes, we are extremely creative. However, many people come up with more than four. When we're getting into the area of ten or more we are incredibly creative; and many people score higher than ten in seminars.

Increasing our creativity

You see, we are creative, but we sometimes do not take the time to be creative. Let's look at the variety of ways we can increase our creativity.

1. Day-dreaming. It is always said that Einstein came up with the theory of relativity while sitting on a grassy bank and imagining riding a sunbeam. I believe we should take time to day-dream. Most of us already do when we're driving, walking or standing by the sea, and perhaps when we're in the bath or shower or simply lying in bed.

Don't be scared to take the time to day-dream. Many successful people say they have had their best ideas when sitting quietly on their own. I once read an article that said it guaranteed success if you would only take half an hour each day to open your mind.

2. Lateral thinking. Edward De Bono, who coined the phrase 'lateral thinking', has some excellent ideas for creative thought.

The 'reverse' idea is very simple. Instead of finding out how we *can* do something, let's find out how we *can't* do it. That will surely show us how we can. For example, years ago I asked the directors of Compass to answer the question, 'How do we pay the salesforce less money?' That may have seemed a strange request but, of course, the reverse of the answer told us how we could pay the salesforce more money. If we were paying the salesforce more money, presumably it was because they were making the company more money.

Write yourself a question on paper and then write down the answers. You know my thoughts about paper: it does not waste time, it uses time effectively.

Edward De Bono, I'm told, came up with the idea of Neighbourhood Watch, by reversing the problem an American city was having with a crime wave. I believe he just said, 'Let's make everybody a policeman.' Isn't that a great idea?

3. The dictionary. Another idea from De Bono is to get the dictionary, open it at any page, stab your finger down and look for the nearest noun. Then try to associate that noun with the particular problem or opportunity. For example, a Japanese TV-manufacturing company wanted an idea to launch a new product, and the word from the dictionary was . . . 'cheese'.

A discussion took place as to how to associate cheese with television. Could we have smellivision? Could televisions be cheese-wedge shaped? No. What else has cheese got that television could have? Well, some cheese have holes. Could a television have holes? If so, what sort of holes? Afterthoughts about holes for speakers, holes for switches, holes in the top of the television for plant pots, etc. The idea was put forward that the screen should have a hole, a hole through which we could see the programmes on different channels. That's how the idea of 'picture in picture' came about, which is now widely available on televisions.

I've used this idea of the dictionary – it's a great deal of fun and works really well.

De Bono has another book called *Six Thinking Hats,* where by wearing a different-colour hat, we have to act in the manner of that hat wearer. For example, black for negative, yellow for sunny, red for emotional, green for creative. I can highly recommend this book. I was so impressed with it I bought six other copies for the directors at Compass and we used it as the basis for our board meetings, to great effect.

What I want you to do now is to write down your most pressing problem. Write it down as a question to yourself. First, write it in reverse and come up with ten solutions. Second, write it down as the problem itself, pick up the dictionary that's on the desk, open it and stab in your finger.

You will find you can always be more creative if you have first set your goals (and we've already discussed how to do that); second, that you have a major problem; or, third, that you write down focused questions to yourself. It's back to the old idea of self-management.

4. Twenty answers. Earl Nightingale, who founded the Nightingale Conant Corporation in America, one of the largest audio-tape suppliers in the world, formulated a creative idea to solve problems. This was to write down a focused question, such as, 'How can I double my sales in the next 12 months?' and then force yourself to write down 20 answers.

Having used this idea I found the first ten were quite simple, the next five were hard, but then I was on a roll again and could come up with five or even ten or more answers to the focused question.

Nightingale's suggestion was to do this three days running, after which you would have a minimum of 60 answers, even though many would be interlinked. I tried this for three days and was amazed how creative I could become.

So again, let's stop to write down that particular question, 'How could I double my sales in the next 12 months?'

5. Dare to be different. We have already mentioned daring to be different: the insurance salesman called Richard who pulled a grenade from his desk, and the other insurance salesman who said: 'I *buy* life insurance.' Let's take some of our more outrageous ideas to see if we could actually make them work. Perhaps we might frighten ourselves with our first offer.

One of the sales letters we use to sell our in-house training courses is entitled 'Once upon a time there were two frogs . . .' It's all about attitude, and I will share it with you later. I'm certain there are not many sales directors or personnel directors who receive letters with that sort of headline. That certainly is daring to be different.

6. Visualisation. When we were discussing goal setting we touched on the area of visualisation, and this can help us again to be more creative. If we visualise the solution, the road to the solution is obvious. Perhaps there is more than one road to get to the destination.

Usually our minds have all the answers. We just need to have a system, like the preceding six ideas, to open our mind and the answers will pop out.

In a selling situation, we can be creative in a variety of areas:

1. What is our best market? What is our worst market?
2. Why do people buy or not buy?
3. Why do people buy from the competition? Could we use competitors' ideas? After all, there are no prizes for originality.
4. How can we offset what the competitors do?
5. Use those six honest serving men: who, why, when, where, what and how.
6. Who are our major competitors?
7. Who are our customers and, more importantly, who aren't our customers?

We can be more creative in the following areas:

1. Finding new customers
2. New product uses
3. New products
4. New sales ideas.

If you believe you are creative, you are creative.

The steps to success

Step 1

Improve your memory by taking a memory course.

Step 2

Improve your product knowledge. Perhaps one of the easiest ways of doing this is to have product-knowledge quizzes at your sales meetings. If you have a reasonably large team, each member of the team can come to the meeting with one product-knowledge question. If you have a small team, each member could come with three or four questions. They are handed to the sales manager, who reads out all the questions. This is a great way to find out who knows what, and it will increase our product knowledge.

Step 3

Do that paper-clip test again, and also with the following items:

(a) A golf ball
(b) A piece of string
(c) A table leg
(d) A sheet of brown paper
(e) A knife.

Step 4

Use the ideas for being more creative in all areas of your life: your sales activities, your leisure activities, general business operation, holiday arrangements, writing mail shots.

On one of the open seminars I ran a lady named Elizabeth attended. She was in the consultancy business dealing with building societies. She wanted to send a mail shot or a sales letter to a number of building societies to invite them to an exhibition. Having discussed how to write a mail shot, which we are going to cover later (Chapter 19), and using the ideas we've just discussed for being creative, Elizabeth wrote a sales letter in the lunchbreak. I looked over it with her and suggested some minor changes. When she returned to her office she sent out the letter in its finished form.

She had created it using the idea of the song, 'The Teddy Bears' Picnic'. She was certainly daring to be different. The response? . . . 21 per cent!

Step 5

Find out about Tony Buzan's and Edward De Bono's books.

Step 6

Open your filter gate by simply saying, 'I am creative.'

Step 7

Regularly review your notes on creative action.

Another test. As a mark out of 100, how creative are you?

CHAPTER 14

Time management

Time management is another of the 'must have' skills for all successful people, particularly those in sales. I once saw in a magazine a story that went as follows. A tramp was sitting on a bench and, going smoothly past him, was a Rolls-Royce. In the back of the Rolls-Royce sat a young man with a glass of brandy in his hand, smoking a long cigar. The young man was dressed in an immaculate suit. The tramp said: 'There but for *me* go I.'

If we do *not* have effective time management we end up frustrated and do *not* perform to the level we know we can. If we think of those who sell advertising space on TV, radio or newspapers, once that slot has gone it can never be sold again. We have to think about our time in that way. Once it's gone, it's gone for ever.

Just look at some of the expressions regarding time:

'Procrastination is the thief of time.'
'Time marches on.'
'If only I had time to . . .'
'Doesn't time fly when you're having fun?'

and of course that old one . . .

'Time and time again.'

In fact, the last one is totally inaccurate. There is no such thing as time and time again. Once we have *spent* time, it will never come back.

Time is the only asset we all have in common and it's how effectively we use our time that will determine how successful we are. There is little point in having all the skills to be successful, having written goals, being creative, knowing how to close sales, if we don't create time to use those skills.

People often say, 'How do you *spend* your time?' Please note the word *spend*. It's just as though it's money and, of course, time *is* money. Let's do another test to see how effectively we're currently using our time.

Time management test

I'm particularly uncomfortable with the words 'always' and 'never', and many of the tests I've seen over the years have included these two words. I've removed them for the sake of this test. Put a tick in the column that's applicable to your answer.

	Often	**Some-times**	**Seldom**
1. Do you write a 'to do' list every day?			
2. Do you prioritise your 'to do' list?			
3. Do you complete all the items on the list?			
4. Is your desk organised and tidy?			
5. Is your filing system up to date?			
6. Do you finish work before the deadline?			
7. Do you put things back in their place?			
8. Do you have up-to-date written goals?			
9. Do you take action daily to achieve them?			
10. Do you handle each piece of paper once only?			
11. Do you start and finish tasks on time?			
12. Do you handle interruptions effectively?			
13. Do you plan for quiet time at work?			
14. Do you plan to prevent problems arising?			

	Often	Some-times	Seldom
15. Are you effective at delegating?			
16. Are people keen to help with work you have delegated to them?			
17. Do you handle talkative telephone callers effectively?			
18. Can you return to your work after an interruption and carry on effectively?			
19. Are you punctual?			
20. Do others know your best time?			
21. Do you do your important work at your best time of day?			
22. Can others cope with your work?			
23. Can you unwind and not worry at home?			
24. Are you making best use of your time?			
25. Are you assertive?			

Scores

Score 4 for often, 2 for sometimes, 0 for seldom.

100–81: you are currently managing your time effectively.

61–80: you usually manage your time effectively, but may be suffering through a lack of consistency.

41–60: you're letting situations take control of your time.

21–40: you're out of control with your time.

0–20: you're probably suffering from stress.

Keep a time log

To know if we can use our time more effectively, we need to find out where we currently spend our time. The way to do this is to keep a time log for one or two days.

If you've never done this I can assure you it is not as easy to do as it first appears. Many of us get caught up in the activities of the day and forget to write down in the relevant section of the time log what we were doing. It works as follows:

Take a piece of ruled paper and, down the left-hand side, write the times for half-hour segments throughout the course of the day. The second, widest column is for the details of what happened in those half-hours. The third column is labelled A, B and C. An example is shown below.

Time log

Name ______________________ **Date** ________________

Time	Details	A/B/C
8.00		
8.30		
9.00		
9.30		
10.00		
10.30		
11.00		
11.30		
12.00		
12.30		

Time	Details	A/B/C
1.00		
1.30		
2.00		
2.30		
3.00		
3.30		
4.00		
4.30		
5.00		
5.30		

_____A hours ______ B hours ____C hours

What I'd like you to do now is to decide on which day you will do a time log. All you do through the course of the day is keep this page in front of you, or in your diary, and, at every half-hour interval (if that's appropriate), you write down what you were doing during that time.

At the end of the day you score the actions using your own score chart. For example, you might put:

A: Actual selling time
B: Travelling time
C: Waste of time

My suggestion is you don't have a scoring chart that goes beyond A, B and C. If you have too many possibilities in scoring the chart, it will be impossible to analyse or at least it will be meaningless. Be extremely hard with yourself if you are in the sales business so that you can see the amount of actual selling time you undertake. Before we move on, decide now that you will do a time log for at least one day of your life.

If we're honest with ourselves, most of us waste some time during the day. Why is that? Now write down five reasons why you waste time:

1. ____________________
2. ____________________
3. ____________________
4. ____________________
5. ____________________

I think we can summarise our answers as follows: negative self-image, low self-esteem, self-doubt, fear of failure, fear of making the wrong decisions, distraction, lack of urgency, non-specific goals, inability to say 'No', lack of control and lack of delegation.

Good time management is all about planning. Remember the six Ps Principle? Proper Planning Prevents Particularly Poor Performance. We have to plan our work and then work the plan.

If we use the 'Yesterday's Road Philosophy' and look at the end result we require, the road there will become obvious. I suggest that at each weekend you plan what you want to achieve for the week. Decide what needs to be done to achieve the result and mark up your diary with the actions. Then simply take the actions. *Why is it that opportunity knocks only once, but temptation keeps banging on the door?*

This idea of 'to do lists' is one of the most effective time-management tools I've ever come across and I use it every day. If you've not used lists before, I suggest you do so.

At the end of each day write down the actions you know you must take the following day. Try to limit this to your five or six major actions. Prioritise that list, put them into order and write them in your diary. Most modern diaries have a space for actions as well as for appointments. When you arrive at work the next day, start item one and keep going until you finish it.

This idea will never make you do less work but has every opportunity of allowing you to achieve more out of every single day. Planning really is the key to good time management. After all, it wasn't raining when Noah built the ark. Plan everything on paper, get feedback by taking actions and then re-adjust the plan.

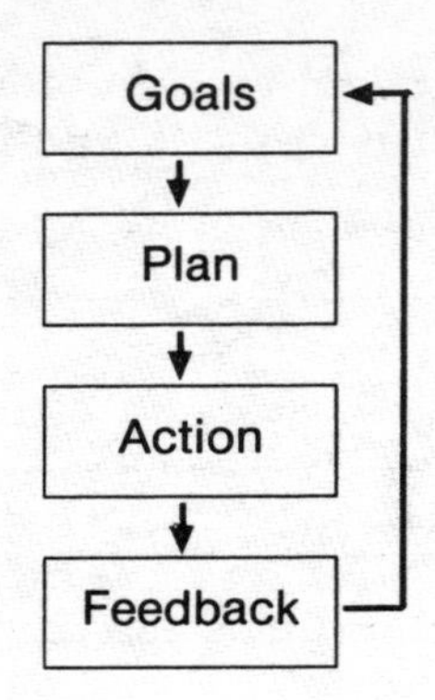

The steps to success

Step 1

Prepare a plan for all aspects of your work:

(a) Time
(b) Customers
(c) Territory
(d) Learning

Step 2

Plan each week in advance and allocate the actions in your diary.

Step 3

Do a time log at least once (preferably one day each month).

Step 4

Analyse the time log and incorporate what you've learnt into your plan.

Step 5

Do 'to do' lists every single day.

Step 6

Become your own manager: remember the mirror theory.

Step 7

If at all possible, work locally. Have you sold to all the customers within a ten-mile radius of your home?

Step 8

Constantly ask yourself, 'Is what I'm doing now making money?' This is what I call the three Ms principle: 'Money Making Movements.'

Step 9

Be realistic:

(a) Work often expands or contracts to the time allocated to its completion.
(b) Everything takes longer than you think.
(c) Don't take on too much.
(d) Plan to use waiting time.

Step 10

Learn to say 'No'. I once heard an idea that suggested the reason we all say 'Yes' too often ('Yes' to evening engagements: 'Yes' to weekend engagements; 'Yes' to daytime engagements) is that we are looking for approval. Our lack of self-esteem prompts us to look for that approval by saying 'Yes' to all the invitations, instead of thinking about it and deciding whether we really want to go.

Having heard this idea, I went to my diary and across every evening for the rest of the year (some four months) I wrote the word 'No'. This did not mean I would say 'No' to every single invitation. It simply reminded me I was capable of saying 'No'. I was amazed how many invitations I didn't accept and, that I didn't miss, and how much more time I had for the important things in my life. Try it.

Step 11

Allocate chunks of time for yourself. One of the people we seldom keep appointments with is ourselves. Yet so often the time spent alone, planning or visualising or setting goals, is some of the most productive time we ever spend. Take out your diary now and make appointments with yourself that are unbreakable.

Step 12

Make a note in your diary to do the self-assessment time-management quiz once a month.

Let me now just cover a couple more ideas on planning, which I'm certain will not only help you with your time management but also with your results.

Preview/Review

The first idea is preview/review, and the way this works is quite simple. Before going into a sales call or a meeting, take just a few minutes in your car and write down a review of the call. It may sound strange to *review* the call rather than *preview* the call, as you haven't actually had the meeting. However, by clearly focusing your mind on the end result as though it had already happened, you create pressures within yourself to make sure the results will be as *you* desire.

Some of the best meetings I have ever had in my commercial career have been those where I've bothered to take the time to do a preview/review.

Only one sale

Imagine the next sales call you are going to make could be the only sales call you could ever make in your life, and that all your future success was dependent on the results of that call.

1. How well planned would you be?
2. Would you have done a preview/review?
3. Would you have practised your opening statement?
4. Would you have tried to be creative?
5. Would you be focusing on benefits for the customer?
6. Would you have allocated the correct amount of time for the meeting?
7. Would you have practised your features and benefits?
8. Would you have practised your negotiation skills?
9. Would you have practised your closing skills?

I'm sure you can think of another 20 questions to add to this list, to all of which you know the answer must be . . . *yes*! If we thought of all our sales calls in this way our successes would dramatically increase.

CHAPTER 15

Telephone techniques

We have already discussed the fact that we must have a prepared opening to our telephone conversations. We have also discussed the word 'picture' and its relevance to our voice: pitch, inflection, courtesy, tone, understandability, rate and enunciation (page 58). We have also discussed preparing a picture-of-a-customer form to be used when we are on the telephone. Let us now, therefore, look at a variety of other ideas.

The work area

It is essential, when we are telephone selling, that our desks or work areas are clear. If we have unnecessary items that will distract us (that letter we must write, that paperwork we must deal with, etc.), we will not be focused firmly on our customers and the benefits of our product or service to them. Either clear the desk or have a separate desk from which you make telephone sales calls.

Type of phone

These days we are all using push-button telephones; however, it is possible to get a computerised system with a call-making facility. If you are aiming to make heavy volumes of outgoing sales calls, this will be an essential part of your equipment.

Picture of a customer

We must prepare a picture-of-a-customer form on which we have listed all the questions we need to ask to gather information before we make our proposal. The form will show the normal closes we will use, together with standard objections and our answers to them.

Goal sheet

If we believe in the saying, 'What you set . . . is what you get', it is essential we set goals for our telephone sales calls.

First, we need to decide on either the number of calls we are going to make or the success we're going to achieve. It is far better to have a success goal than a simple performance goal. Decide that your telephone activity will achieve three sales before you stop or three appointments before you stop rather than you will work for 45 minutes. Setting a results or achievement goal does not mean you cannot stop for coffee or lunch.

We need to decide the goal of the sales call: it may be a sale, an appointment, take referrals, sort out a problem or arrange delivery. The list can be endless; however, if we don't decide before we make the call what the goal is, we have little chance of accomplishing it.

Customer record sheet

We discuss in full customer records in Chapter 16. It is vital we have our customer record sheet or file on our desk when making a call so we can update immediately that customer record from the information we gather during a telephone conversation.

Mirror

I have always believed it's a good idea to have a mirror on a telephone sales desk so we can self-manage our activity and 'psych' up before we make the call by smiling at ourselves.

Records

The other records we need to keep are the number of calls we make and the successes we achieve. It's only by keeping these records that we will be able to undertake projections for our future success. Knowing how many calls it takes to achieve one sale or one appointment will assist us in all stages of planning for increased business.

Referrals

We will need our referral cards, either in printed form or blank 3 x 5 cards, stacked on our desk as a constant reminder to ask for referrals on every possible occasion.

By referrals I mean the names of other potential customers your current customers give you. When asking for referrals we mustn't say: 'Do you know anybody else who could use us?' We must have a prepared and planned referral question.

If we ask 'Do you know anybody else . . .' we are asking customers to search the whole of their memory banks to come up with names. What we need to do is to phrase questions that will make the customers think of a particular sector of their experience or memory banks so they can focus in on two or three customers to give as their referrals. For example: 'I'm certain you know other people who are involved in selling?'

The customer answers 'Yes'.

'Do you know any sales managers?'

The customer answers 'Yes'.

'Do you know any sales directors?'

The customer answers 'Yes'.

'As I know you're pleased with the service we've been providing to you and your company, you wouldn't have a problem if I contacted them using your name, would you?'

The customer answers 'That's fine.'

'These sales managers and directors we were thinking about, then, what are their names and phone numbers?'

You see how you'll be able to work with this, to blend it into your type of business. You really can focus the customers' minds using the technique of 'did you do Latin' on to the specific names of customers they can give you as referrals.

Telephone recording

These days it's possible to buy approved equipment you can connect to your telephone line to record your own telephone calls. This is an excellent idea, as few of us have the type of memory that enables us to recall every single word uttered during a conversation. If you arrange this in your company, I suggest you set up one or two rules:

1. That the tape with the recorded call belongs to the person whose voice is on the tape.
2. That no copies are taken of the tape.
3. That the tape is played in front of other people only with the permission of the person whose voice is being recorded.

These simple and courteous rules will ensure we're not embarrassed recording our telephone calls, thinking they're likely to be played at an office party or in the director's car on the way home.

Recording telephone calls can be a terrific training device as we are able to spot potential closing opportunities, mistakes we've made, things we said correctly and can use again and, perhaps, even information the customer provided that we missed the first time round.

You will easily find a telephone recording device advertised. It will be one of the miscellaneous items for sale in magazines.

Getting past the gatekeeper

How do we get to speak to the buyer? We all know this difficulty, don't we? The receptionist who is determined we will not pass. I heard an excellent idea recently that we no longer call them receptionists but rejectionists!

Then there are those secretaries who believe they are wardens to their bosses instead of their assistants. I'm sure you've found that, where you get a hard receptionist and a very hard secretary, the boss is usually reasonable. Where you get through very easily, the boss is able to take care of him or herself.

There is little new in the art of getting past receptionists and secretaries, but let me examine the basic ideas:

1. We need to be firm but pleasant.
2. We need to ask for the customer by name and, if the first name is known, by repeating the first name in the following way: 'John . . . John Smith, please.'
3. We can use the idea of 'Will you please tell John Smith that Peter Thomson is on the phone for him?'
4. Send a letter before the telephone call making reference to the fact that you will be calling.
5. Use a technique called 'click whirr'. This is based on the idea that certain words throw a switch in our brains and put them into motion. The switch goes click and the wheels start to turn with a whirring noise.

   Recent studies show that 'I need . . . because . . .' is a click-whirr technique. Studies were done with queues waiting to use a photo-copier. When people came to the queue, and tried to push in at the front, there was obviously annoyance. However, when people came and said, 'I *need* to use the photo-copier now *because* . . .' the people in the queue gladly obliged. This research indicated that it was totally irrelevant which words followed the 'because'. The 'I need . . . *because* . . .was sufficient a click-word technique for people to agree.

   We can use this in our telephone sales calls by saying: 'I need to speak to Mr Smith because . . .', adding whatever is relevant to your business.

   You can use the click-whirr technique of 'I need . . . because . . .' when asking for a discount – ie., 'I need a discount because I never pay retail,' 'I need a discount because . . .'

If you are having extreme difficulty getting past the rejectionist to speak to the buyer, you might try the following idea. Phone the company, get the buyer's name, put down the receiver. Later in the day phone again and ask for the stores or accounts department. When you get through to stores or accounts, ask them to transfer to you the buyer – asking for the buyer's extension number at the same time. While this is not the best approach to make in a new situation, you may at least get the buyer's secretary and be able to send information or arrange an appointment that way.

One salesman was so frustrated in trying to get an appointment with the buyer that he finally sent the buyer a cake, with a message piped on top in blue icing, saying: 'I'm going to call you at 4.05 pm. Please speak to me.'

Some years ago, two members of my salesforce were struggling. We thought we'd tried everything – most of their activity was by telephone and yet whatever training we gave them they simply didn't seem to be able to succeed.

In desperation I tried the following idea. I said to them: 'What I want you to do now is to go and make some more telephone calls to get 20 people to say "No! I won't see you". I want you to be so positive, so full of benefits, so over the top with the customer, there is not a hope in hell anybody will agree to see you. In fact, the more people who say, "No! I don't want to give you an appointment", the happier I will be. Go off and do it now.'

Off the two men went, full of enthusiasm for this new idea of 'upsetting the customers'. Within half an hour they were both back, wearing rueful smiles, realising they'd been had and with details of the three appointments they had both achieved.

The steps to success

Step 1

Have a clear work area.

Step 2

Use the right type of phone.

Step 3

Prepare a picture-of-a-customer form, including the closes, objections and questions.

Step 4

Have a goal sheet.

Step 5

Maintain acccurate records.

Step 6

Have a prepared opening statement.

Step 7

'Psych up' before the call.

Step 8

Be determined to succeed.

Step 9

Set a target for a success goal, not just a performance goal.

Step 10

Record your calls.

CHAPTER 16

Keeping records

It's always been said that the salespeople who keep records are the salespeople who break records. It's only by keeping records that we know what customers have ordered, what they might order and a vast variety of other information that will assist us in our sales careers.

Let's break down our customer records into two major areas: first, the 'windows of opportunity' and, second, a list of those headings we will need to compile a customer record form.

The windows of opportunity

This is an excellent idea that was explained to me a long time ago by the sales manager of a national company. I have used the idea, worked with it and found it to be an excellent time saver and an excellent way to increase sales and profits.

It is based on the idea that it costs about seven times more to sell a product to a new customer than it does to sell a product to an existing customer. What I'd like you to do is to draw the diagram at the top of page 160. We have the same diagram filled in below it.

Down the left-hand side write the names of ten of your customers. Along the bottom of the grid write six of the products or services you sell. I've only picked six products and ten customers at this stage because I'm sure you'll be able to do this from memory.

Now colour in the meeting square, where a customer's name meets a product or service that customer buys. The holes left are our windows of opportunity with our current customer base.

Certain customers may be unable to use one of your services or products because they simply don't fit the customer's requirements. If that is the case, colour in that meeting square. We should still be left with a tremendous number of windows of opportunity.

When you are in your office I would like you to arrange a list of all your customers and a list of all your products so that you can complete a major diagram for your opportunities. If your customer list or client list is extremely long, you may have to prepare this on a computer. This can be done quite easily with a spreadsheet software package.

If you're involved in sales management and want projections for a

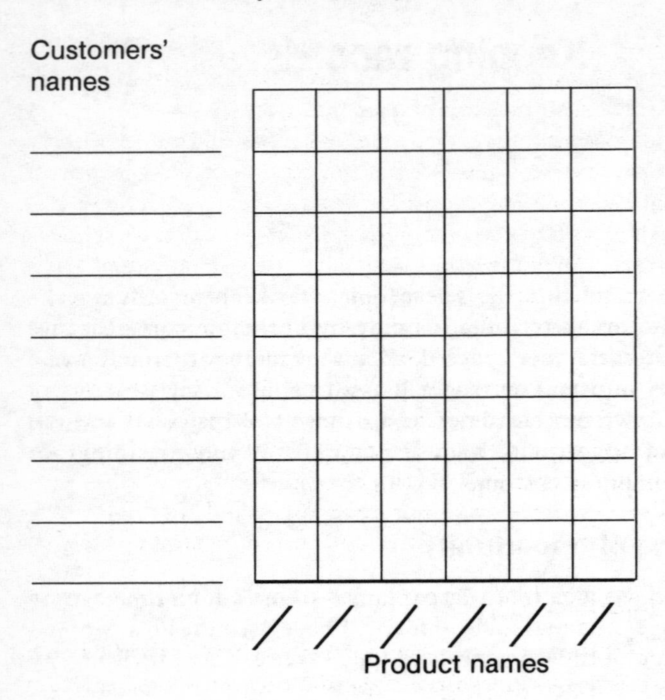
Customers' names
Product names

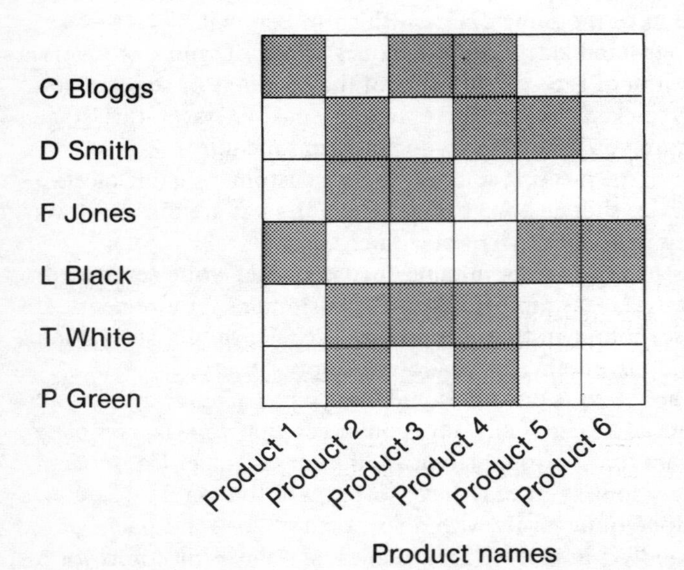
C Bloggs
D Smith
F Jones
L Black
T White
P Green
Product 1
Product 2
Product 3
Product 4
Product 5
Product 6
Product names

particular area or if, as a member of a salesforce, you are asked for projections for your own area, you can use this windows of opportunity graph to establish potential future turnover.

By making telephone calls to your customers to find out the likely date they will order the services listed at the bottom of the graph, you can even prepare a month-by-month or year-by-year projection.

You may wish to add to the bottom-line list of products or services the word 'referrals' to prompt you to ask customers on a regular basis for referrals. Don't just have one line for referrals, have a number.

The additional advantage of the windows of opportunity graph is this. Let's say, for example, you have 200 customers and you decide to add a new product to your range. Suddenly you have 200 more windows of opportunity. Conversely, you may have a range of 20 products and you obtain five new customers, each of whom buy only one product. Suddenly you have another 95 windows of opportunity.

The graph, while extremely simple to prepare and use, can really focus our minds on the potential from our current customer base.

Customer record

I'm now going to share with you a list of items I believe should be on a customer record form. Some of them will be obvious, some of them less so. They are a compilation of my own experiences and the various books and record systems I've seen over the years:

- Company name.
- Address.
- Post code.
- Telephone number.
- Fax number.
- Type of business.
- Parent company.
- Subsidiary company.
- Number of staff.
- Turnover.
- SIC (Standard Industry Code).
- A list of the potential benefits of your products to customers obtained by asking your current customer base why they buy your products.
- Name of the decision-makers and the decision-influencers (possibly secretary or user of product), including:

    (a) full name;
    (b) job title;

(c) telephone numbers and extensions;
(d) habits (drinker, non-drinker and likes)
(e) smoker, non-smoker;
(f) birthday;
(g) family details;
(h) hobbies (together with as many other personal items such those listed above as you can find out);
(i) hot buttons;
(j) ordering frequency;
(k) auditory/visual/kinesthetic.

- Accounts information.
- Name of the person who arranges payment.
- The payment terms that have been agreed.
- Person who agreed them and the date they were agreed.
- Delivery details.
- Addresses of branch offices.
- Special instructions from customer.
- Customer's ordering procedure.
- Details of potential in-house referrals.
- Details of referrals taken and success rate for out-house referrals.
- Windows of opportunity graph, specifically for each customer.
- Your plan for the development of the customer.

I am certain you could probably add a variety of other headings to go with this form but the above list certainly is comprehensive and covers the main ideas. Within your customer file you will also keep copies of correspondence together with copies of items of interest you have actually sent to the customer.

The steps to success

Step 1

Design and print an in-house sales-record customer file. As desk-top publishing software is readily available at inexpensive prices, most companies can have a personalised customer-record form.

Step 2

If your business needs many copies of the record forms, I suggest you contact one of the major sales-record companies, such as Kalamazoo plc of Birmingham.

Step 3

Write to your customers regularly to update them on new items of importance, and keep copies of the correspondence in the file.

Step 4

Ensure you deal with all the departments in each of your customer companies.

Step 5

Decide to use customer records as your score-card for success. Remember . . . the salespeople who keep records are the salespeople who break records.

Notes

Topic

Action plan

Name ______________________________

Topic ______________________ **Date** __________

Action	Target date	Completion date
1.		
2.		
3.		
4.		
5.		
6.		

CHAPTER 17

Rejection analysis

Self-analysis is one of the major strengths of successful people. However, if we do analyse we sometimes only look at our mistakes – the negative things or what went wrong. While this is important it is also essential to analyse our good points, the positives and the things that went right, so we can repeat them again and again.

One of the easiest ways to increase our success in selling is to undertake this idea of the preview/review: writing down what's going to happen and, after the call, reviewing your thoughts to see if you actually achieved the goals you set out.

Keeping score keeps us on track and creates a pressure to perform. Our discussions on goal setting should be used during your self-analysis time.

Salesperson analysis

Score one point for each 'Yes' answer:

1. Do I have written goals for my sales activity and my self-development?
2. Do I prepare goals for each sales call?
3. Do I have written goals for the development of each customer?
4. Do I plan each sales call in advance?
5. Have I, or my company, undertaken market research to target those areas of the market that will meet our objectives?
6. Do I keep up-to-date records regarding the number of calls to interviews, and the number of interviews to sales, etc?
7. Do I have a prepared opening statement?
8. Do I have prepared questions to find out client needs?
9. Do I ask questions in such a way that customers will give me all the information I need?
10. Do I spend the maximum amount of time each day actually selling?
11. Do I design creative solutions to sales problems?
12. When customers explain their needs, do I verify my understanding of them?

13. Do I sell benefits and results, not just features?
14. Do I respond to customers' objections in a calm and professional manner?
15. Do I summarise the customer's needs and how my product will benefit the customer before asking for the order?
16. Do I close clearly and calmly?
17. When I have taken an order, do I explain clearly to the customer what will happen next?
18. Do I check with customers after delivery of the service or product to ensure they have received what they ordered?
19. Do I maintain regular contact with my customers?
20. Do I analyse my strengths and weaknesses?

Scores

15–20: Well done! Keep analysing and taking action.

9–14: Not bad, but spend more time on planning to increase your results.

8 and under: Reassess your sales activity and spend a great deal more time on planning.

Another excellent way to undertake a self-analysis of our sales activity is to use a chart similar to the one opposite.

The way we use the chart is as follows. Down the left-hand side you will see the numbers 1–20, and these relate to 20 likely reasons why you did not obtain a sale. Over the course of a three-week period, mark in after each unsuccessful sales call, by way of a tick, your thoughts as to why you did not make the sale. When the three-week period has passed, you will have an excellent chart showing clearly the areas on which you need to work.

Make certain you complete the chart after every unsuccessful call, as trying to do it at the end of the day will be far less effective. Be totally honest with yourself; the purpose of self-analysis is to improve your results. If you find the chart works for you, as I'm sure it will, maintain it as a regular part of your record-keeping system.

A list of the 20 likely reasons for unsuccessful sales is given overleaf. You may decide that you wish to add others and will therefore extend the chart, or that some of my thoughts are not relevant to your business – in which case delete them and insert those reasons that are applicable. I saw a chart like this in a magazine years ago and thought it a great idea.

	M	T	W	T	F	M	T	W	T	F	M	T	W	T	F
1															
2															
3															
4															
5															
6															
7															
8															
9															
10															
11															
12															
13															
14															
15															
16															
17															
18															
19															
20															

Reasons for failure to sell

1. I had a negative attitude and showed it.
2. I didn't listen actively and talked far too much.
3. I failed to spot the hot button.
4. I explained items about my product or service but the customer didn't believe me.
5. I argued with the customer.
6. My presentation was unenthusiastic.
7. I didn't listen carefully to objections and interrupted the customer with my answers.
8. After the first refusal I gave up.
9. I didn't establish who made the decision to buy.
10. I didn't tell the customer anything interesting or new or give any reasons to buy.
11. I forgot to talk about benefits and only mentioned features.
12. I failed to get agreement to each point as I moved forward in the presentation.
13. I didn't understand quite how the customer was going to use our products.
14. I made the presentation far too complicated.
15. I fell down in product knowledge.
16. I didn't realise some of the objections were spurious.
17. I didn't isolate the objection so that I could close when I had dealt with it.
18. I failed to deal with interruptions effectively.
19. I spent far too much time on general conversation and not business.
20. I didn't ask for the order or close the sale.

Before we move on to the rejection part of this particular project, let's look at some of the steps we can take to increase our skill at analysis.

The steps to success

Step 1

Always preview/review.

Step 2

Use the reasons-for-failure chart to analyse your weaknesses.

Step 3

Do a review after every call.

Step 4

Get into the habit of analysing on paper, with goals, before every sales call.

Step 5

Each week become your own sales manager and analyse the week.

Step 6

Be aware of analysis paralysis. While it is an excellent idea to undertake analysis, we must make sure there is sufficient time to take action as well. After all, you didn't interview every candidate before you got married.

Rejection

The fear of rejection holds most of us back from achieving the level of success our level of skill indicates we should achieve.

Why do we fear rejection? If customers didn't reject salespeople's proposals we wouldn't need salespeople. Did you get into a selling career believing there would be no rejections? Of course you didn't. You know it's the price we have to pay. If customers would simply beat a path to our doors and place the orders, none of us in sales would have a job. Rejection is simply a step along the path to success.

Imagine I had in my pocket a list of 50 names of customers who had been researched, and 90 per cent of them were guaranteed to buy. Would you want that list? Of course you would. However, there is a catch. You can only have the list for 24 hours and you can't take photo-copies. Do you still want it? Yes? OK, in that case, please answer these questions:

1. When would you start work on it?
2. Would you take a lunch-break?
3. Would you take coffee breaks?
4. What time would you finish in the evening?

The only difference between this list and any other list is that the fear of rejection has been taken away. Isn't that right?

We must look on rejection as a learning opportunity: it's that old saying that a block of granite in the path of the weak is a stumbling block; in the path of the strong it's simply a stepping-stone.

By using all the rejections we come across, all the 'nos', all the 'I don't wants', all those failed appointments, we can learn why we failed and do our utmost to ensure we succeed next time.

Let's look at some famous people in history. It was said of Enrico Caruso, when he first started to sing, that his voice was like wind whistling through a window. Of Benjamin Disraeli that, when he gave his first speech in Parliament, people hissed and laughed. Disraeli responded with: 'Though I sit down now, the time will come when you will hear me.' Marconi said that Heinrich Hertz's discoveries could be applied to worldwide wireless communications. He was informed this was contrary to the laws of physics. Christopher Columbus was told he'd fall off the edge of the world.

When George Orwell sent his book, *Animal Farm,* to the publishers, it was returned with a note saying it was impossible to sell animal stories in the USA. The review from one of the publishers who received William Golding's book, *Lord of the Flies,* responded: 'It does not seem to us that you have been wholly successful in working out an admittedly promising idea.' Finally, Jeffrey Archer, one of the most well-known authors of modern times, had his first book, *Not a Penny More, Not a Penny Less,* rejected 17 times.

Therein lies the key *we* need to calculate how many rejections, how may steps it's going to take to get one sale – how many phone calls it's going to take to get an appointment, how many appointments to take an order.

If we know the price we have to pay, and are determined to pay it, we will take the 'nos' gladly, as simply the fact we are closer to achievement.

If, in the past, you've not kept careful records that enable you to analyse how many phone calls to appointment, how many appointments to sale, you will have difficulty calculating the price. If this has been the case with you, I suggest you immediately start keeping those records. If in the past you have kept those records, analyse them so you know the figures. Use the steps-to-success chart.

Steps-to-success chart

1. Set an income goal for the next 12 months £ __________
2. Divide by four, equals quarterly income goal £ __________
3. Deduct basic salary, equals commission requirement £ __________
4. Average commission per sale equals £ __________
5. Divide (3) by (4), equals number of sales required __________
6. Number of appointments to achieve one sale __________

7. (6) times (5) equals total appointments required ___________
8. Number of telephone calls to obtain one appointment ___________
9. (8) times (7) equals total number of phone calls to be made per quarter ___________
10. Divide 13, equals number of telephone calls to be made each week ___________
11. Divide by 5, equals total number of telephone calls to be made each day, while allowing time to go on the appointments obtained. ___________

Fear of rejection

How are we going to deal with the fear? I saw it once written that fear is an acronym:

F false
E evidence
A appearing
R real.

It really means that we're worrying about what could happen; that we're mentally rehearsing disaster.

Let's enjoy being scared, let's break our fear down into bite-sized pieces rather in the way we use the salami principle to avoid procrastination. What really is the worst that could happen with your fears? Take time to think about it. Conquer those fears one by one – after all, the longest journey starts with one step.

When customers say 'no' it's not usually *no* to you, it's just *no* to your proposal.

More steps to success

Step 7

Calculate how many steps you need to take using the steps-to-success chart or a customised version of it to achieve the success you desire.

Step 8

Calculate the price of success or, perhaps more importantly, the price of failure. By this I mean, are you going to have to spend less time with your family because of the monetary goals *you* have decided upon?

Step 9

Decide to pay the price.

Step 10

Use the analysis charts to find out why you were rejected and how you will improve next time.

Step 11

Maintain a positive attitude. If you remind yourself how good you are, and that it was only the proposal that was rejected and not you, you will be able to maintain your positive attitude.

Step 12

Welcome fear. Analyse it. Overcome it by the simple application of the skills you already possess.

Step 13

Increase your product knowledge. This will reduce the fear of making mistakes regarding the product or service and its application.

Step 14

Prepare a list of your common rejections and how you will overcome them. Here are some you might come across:

- *I'm not interested.* 'Mr Customer, I can understand that you're not interested. How could you possibly be interested until you know how we might be able to help you? All I need is a few minutes of your time.'
- *I've never heard of your company.* 'Mr Customer, that's why I've called.'
- *I always buy from. . .* 'They are a good company, but we're different, and I'd like a few minutes to explain why.'
- *I'm far too busy to see you.* 'Mr Customer, I've always found that busy people are the successful people. All I need is ten minutes . . .'

Step 15

Write down one or more fears you've conquered in your life. Work out how you conquered them and then apply the same principles to conquer your other fears.

CHAPTER 18

Image

It's said that you can't judge a book by its cover, but most of us do most of the time, and I'm absolutely convinced all our customers do. In fact, customers judge you, the company, the product, after-sales activity, in fact everything . . . by you. They judge by your car, (if they can see it), they judge by your briefcase, your business card, your samples and your brochures.

Customers' likes and dislikes

A recent study said that customers do and do not like the following:

Dos

1. Sales people who have good product knowledge
2. Sales people who are presentable
3. Sales people who are courteous to all the customer's staff
4. Sales people who are honest
5. Sales people who are obviously sincere.

Do nots

1. Flattery
2. Sales people who overstay their welcome
3. Sales people who talk too much
4. Sales people who don't keep promises
5. Sales people who argue.

We are all aware that people buy people before they buy the product. What I'd like you to do now is to complete this short ten-question test.

The effects of image

1. Do I start all my conversations on a positive note?
2. Do I handle my products and brochures with pride?
3. Do I psych up before every call?
4. Do I wear a different suit or set of clothes every day?
5. Do I use matching handshakes?

6. Do I smile?
7. Do I keep my briefcase clean and tidy?
8. Do I polish my shoes every day?
9. Do I keep my brochures and paperwork clean and tidy?
10. Do I keep my car clean and tidy?

These days, with solicitors and accountants able to act like businesses instead of institutions by advertising their services, everyone is in business. So whether a person is professional or not is no longer determined by the business they are involved in, but rather *the way* they are in business.

Appearance is also concerned with your body language, which we discussed earlier, but to exude the right attitude we need to psych ourselves up before every call. It may be we'll use 'I like myself', which was discussed in Chapter 2.

Getting our attitude right means understanding that the grass isn't greener on the other side: it's greener where it's watered. Keep watering your attitude.

The steps to success

Step 1

Either use the test above on a regular basis or design your own self-assessment test on appearance. Check daily that you really do appear as a professional.

I heard a story about a man who went to a railway station, dressed in a suit but *without* a tie. He stopped passers-by and explained to them he'd lost his wallet and would they give him some money to go home. During the course of the experiment he collected £20. The same man then went to a different railway station but this time he wore his tie. He stopped passers-by with the same story, but collected £120.

Isn't it amazing how one small piece of cloth can make all the difference to our believability? Perception is obviously more important than reality.

Step 2

Check your car and briefcase before every call.

Step 3

Give out lots of clean business cards.

Step 4

Invest in your wardrobe: you'll never make a better investment.

Step 5

Psych up before every call.

Step 6

Do not smell of drink or smoke. Do not use bad language, do not be a big head, do not be a non-stop comedian and, more important than anything else, do not be a person with a negative mental attitude. If we take care of our appearance and image, we will be delighted that our customers judge the book by the cover.

CHAPTER 19

Writing sales letters

Like most of the areas we have been covering, the key to success in this topic, writing letters – be they mail shots, sales quotes or any type of writing at all – is . . . planning. The six Ps Principle, Proper Planning Prevents Particularly Poor Performance, applies.

We are going to tackle two different types of letter: mail shots and sales follow-ups.

1. *Mail shots.* My definition of a mail shot is a letter sent to a customer regarding a product or service that asks the customer to buy. It is not a letter following an appointment. The letter may be sent to a current customer or to a potential customer.

2. *Sales quotations letters.* This is a letter sent after a meeting or telephone call to confirm the points discussed and to prompt the customer to buy our products or services.

For both these letters we need to ask ourselves the question: 'What do I want the letter to do?'

With a mail shot it could be that we're looking for a high response to our suggestions that our customers receive further information or brochures. Or we could be looking for a low response but an immediate high conversion rate to order from the letter.

With our sales quotations letters we may want the customers to phone us back to place an order, or we may want the customers to wait for a phone call or something totally different.

So, our first step must be to decide the results we want the letter to achieve.

Mail shots

Let's ask ourselves the following questions:

1. What results do we want?
2. Who are we going to send the letter to?
3. Where will we get the names of those potential customers? It's always said that the list we use is at least 50 per cent of the potential success.

4. What records are we going to keep?
5. How are we going to test the list?
6. What reply device will we use? Phone, card, both? Order form, message service, answering machine, fax?

The following is how we write the actual mail shot letter, and it's an idea I picked up from a free Post Office publication. It described a system called 'WISCDAR'. Those letters stand for the following words:

W wavelength
I interest
S sell benefits
C add conviction
D desire
A action
R result.

I will explain them as follows.

Wavelength. The first line of our mail shot needs to make sure the customer realises we are on the same wavelength. We do that by asking a question, followed by a 'yes tag'. For example: 'It would be marvellous if we were able to end the working day without headaches from the fluorescent lights . . . wouldn't it?'

I'm sure you'll see the idea behind this and will be able to personalise it to a major benefit of your product.

Interest. Our next few words must prompt interest in our particular product or service by explaining in brief terms the details of our offer.

Next, *sell the benefits.* We have discussed at some length the difference between features and benefits. This is our opportunity to sell clearly those major benefits to the recipient of the letter. In many cases with a mail shot you will not know precise information about the potential customer. However, we will have a general feeling for the customer's situation by careful selection of mailing lists, and will therefore be able to sell what we believe to be the *relevant* benefits.

Conviction. It is understandable that potential customers receiving a letter out of the blue may be somewhat sceptical of our ability to provide the product or service concerned, and the value or quality of the product. If we were able to add in to this conviction part of the letter such things as testimonials from well-known companies or people, or a paragraph that clearly convinces the potential customer we are more than able to supply the product to give the benefits concerned, we will obviously increase our chances of success with the letter.

Desire. We obviously need to create a desire within the customer for the product, and we do this by a variety of different response-enhancement techniques, which I'll detail later.

The A stands for *action,* and we must make it simple for the customer to take action by deciding in our planning stage which reply device we will use. The possibilities are as follows:

1. *Phone.* We can ask our customers to telephone their orders, in which case we need to state clearly the telephone number in the action part of the letter.
2. *Card.* It's always been said that a mail shot without a reply-paid card is not a mail shot, and I've had a great deal of success with reply-paid cards. I've had responses on a small mail shot (under 100 names) as high as 48 per cent and on a large mail shot as high as 14 per cent both using the ideas contained in this WISCDAR formula and a reply-paid card.
3. *Both.* We may be able to ask customers either to phone or send back the reply-paid card.
4. With certain products or services it will be possible to include an *order form* with the sales letter that simply needs to be completed and put in the envelope provided.

   There is an important point here: check the order form will fold and fit in the envelope. While this seems pretty obvious, I've received mail shots where the order form doesn't fit the envelope without a great deal of folding.

   Make sure the order form is simple to complete. We often get only one chance for a customer to place an order in response to a mail-shot letter. If it's a complicated order form, the customer may well put the order form down, move on to do something easier and never return to it. In mail shots it's always said that 'later' means 'never'.
5. *Message service.* I've used this idea by employing a message service that provides a special telephone number you can quote in letters. Customers then telephone the message service and either leave their order, their request for information or simply their name and address for a call back. The message service transmits that information to a paging device, or by phone or fax.

   I tried a mail shot using a message service, stating clearly within the letter that the customers would be phoning such a service. The response was excellent.

6. *Answering machine.* It would be possible to ask customers to respond to your mail shot by phoning a specific telephone number. Your letter should state clearly that there will be a recorded announcement, message or facility for placing orders. I deal with a company in America that exports all over the world, and it uses this idea to great effect.

   There have always been problems with people leaving messages on answering machines, but I'm certain this is when they expect someone to answer the phone and they're not prepared to talk to a machine. If, on the other hand, they telephone the number knowing full well there will be a machine to answer the call, they invariably leave their message.

   The same psychology applies to quoting a *fax machine* number.

The R stands for *result,* and its purpose is to ensure we again check we are writing a letter that will achieve the results we require.

Mailing lists

In these days of electronic storage and retrieval where virtually every office in the world has a computer, mailing lists in standard format are easily obtained.

In all the commercial countries of the world there are associations of list brokers and owners. In the United Kingdom it is the Direct Marketing Association. Their address is

Haymarket House
1 Oxendon Street
London SW1Y 4EE
Tel No: 071-321 2525

The DMA has taken over from the British List Brokers Association and will be able to provide a list of all brokers and owners.

I have obtained that list, contacted all the people and now have a major 'list of lists'. I cannot stress enough how important the right list will be to the success of your mail shot.

It's possible to obtain a list of almost anyone who does or has almost anything. I strongly suggest you use the services of a well-known list broker. This help, which is invaluable, will cost you absolutely nothing, as the broker earns commission from the list owner on the rental prices of the list. The list broker will be able to suggest lists and give advice on timings of mailings and the up-to-date discount rates available from the postal service.

With the instant availability of software packages with a mail-merge facility, it is a simple matter to personalise our outgoing letters with the potential customer's name, address and salutation.

I am not a great believer in the over-personalisation of letters, with people's names appearing through the text. I know when I receive letters that have been prepared in this way, and I feel I have been 'merged'.

Records

Our long-term success and failure with mail shots will be determined by the quality of the records we keep. I suggest you keep records that give details as follows:

1. The list that was used
2. The number of letters sent
3. How they were sent
4. A copy of the letter used
5. A copy of any enclosures, such as brochures or reply-paid cards
6. The date sent
7. Details of the replies received and dates
8. Conversion to orders
9. Total costs and breakdown of costs
10. Total income
11. Profit achieved.

Many companies who try mail shots for the first time give up when they receive the usually low response rate of 1 or 2 per cent. I believe this is because they have not realised that obtaining the customers' names or first orders is only the start of the profit calculation.

I have sent many mail shots and, in terms of the first-response income, at best produced a break-even and, on occasions, even a small loss. However, as we all know, this is not the end of the game, it is only the beginning.

Proper use of the responded names and the 'windows of opportunity' chart, together with an effective referral collection system, will ensure that even the lowest of mail-shot responses can be turned into a handsome profit.

Testing

The three golden rules of being involved in the mail-shot business are: test, test and test again.

We need to test all the lists we are aiming to use. Many mailing houses will only sell you a minimum quantity of 5,000 names. It may be better to test 1,000 of those names and then, having produced no results whatsoever, throw away the remaining 4,000 rather than waste all your costs on stamps, letters and brochures. You will certainly need to roll out a test of 1,000, 5,000 and perhaps even 10,000 before running a major mail-shot campaign, sending 50,000 or 100,000 letters.

If you are aiming to undertake a major campaign, using a names list of, say, 50,000, then I would suggest you do a test on 5,000 names, asking the broker or mailing house for what is termed '*n*th selection'. This means that, if you are requesting 5,000 out of 50,000, you'll be supplied with every tenth name on the list. This should ensure you are not concentrating your first test mailer in any particular geographical area or other influencing factor.

Other factors

Some of the research on mail shots indicates that the following three ideas can dramatically increase response rates:

1. Post your mailings so they will arrive on Tuesday morning.
2. Ensure that all your letter mailings are signed in blue.
3. Every letter mailing must, repeat must, have a PS. Research indicates that, when most people receive a letter, they read the headline. They then start to read the letter and immediately move to see who the letter is from, reading the signature and anything close to the signature. The PS must, therefore, state the major benefits and factors of the offer, together with a call for action.

The steps to success

Step 1

Plan everything properly.

Step 2

Write the letter. If you decide to use a mailing house, they will need to see a copy of the letter before they will agree to your using their list.

Step 3

Read the letter and reread the letter to ensure that the grammar, punctuation and spelling are correct.

Step 4

Test, test and test again.

Step 5

Keep excellent records.

Step 6

If you're mailing to sell a product directly off the letter, use a selection from the following list of response-enhancement techniques by Dan Lee Dimke.

1. Offer a free gift. This must be relevant to your offer.
2. Offer a quantity discount. This will plant the idea of a multiple purchase in the customer's mind.
3. Always offer a money-back guarantee and make sure it's stated in bold language with a border round it.
4. A limited-time offer can create urgency. The offer must be believable – the customer will lose a benefit by inaction.
5. Offer a sample at a reduced cost.
6. Use the words 'free' and 'information'. This can be a powerful technique, as these seem to be two of the highest-response pulling words that can be used. You will, of course, need a good follow-up package to send in response to the customer's request.
7. Offer additional supplies. It may be possible to make your company a 'one-stop shop' for all the customer's needs in this particular area.
8. Offer a special bonus with quantity. This needs to be an item that cannot be bought separately.
9. Accept all credit cards if this is appropriate to the value of the goods you sell.
10. Use 24-hour telephone ordering. As discussed earlier, have an answering machine on a dedicated line and state clearly within the letter that this is how customers could order. This could, of course, be a dedicated fax line.
11. If you're selling business to business, offer a 30-day trial of the product. You'll need to be particularly careful with this and weigh up the pros and cons and potential loss.
12. Promise to send the goods the same day. This costs you nothing extra and indicates excellent service.

Sales quotations letter

The first question we need to ask ourselves when sending a sales quotations letter is, 'What are we trying to achieve?' Do we want to use the letter to prompt the customer into responding with an order or to make the customer want to order but to wait until we telephone to take the order or for an appointment? Careful thought will, as always, make sure we write the letter with the appropriate goal in mind.

What to do

1. Plan the sales letter on paper before writing the final draft.
2. Avoid Victoriana.
3. When writing sales quotations letters, use the following formula:

   (a) *Summary.* Summarise the whole letter at the start, to make it easier for the customer to read. This is based on the idea of the TV programme *Columbo.* In most murder-mystery programmes or books we do not find out who the killer is until the last page.

   Columbo has turned this idea on its head by telling us at the start who the murderer is and then going on to solve the mystery. I am sure you have found, as I have, that it is easier to watch *Columbo* because you know 'who dunnit'.

   (b) State the *problem* or *situation* in which the customers currently find themselves. This is based on the fact that, if there is no cavity there is no filling.

   (c) Make your *proposal* for the solution.

   (d) Explain the *costs,* including payment terms.

   (e) Follow this with the *benefit* and, if applicable, use a balance-sheet approach showing how the benefits more than outweigh the costs.

   (f) *Conclusion.* This will clearly state how you arrived at your conclusion based on the problem or situation, the solution, the costs and the benefits.

   (g) *The close.* In exactly the same way as we would close in a face-to-face or a telephone sales situation, we must close in our letters. Leaving the customer hanging on the end of the letter by not asking for an order will not produce the sales we require from these quotations.

   (h) *What to do now.* In my sales letters I put the heading 'What to do now' and then go on to explain clearly and politely the actions the customer needs to take to enjoy the benefits of the goods or services I am providing. I've found that this works extremely well and suggest you use it.

4. *Present it well.* A little bit of extra time and cost to present our proposals in the most professional way possible will be time and money well spent. Customers like to deal with other professionals.

Let's show them how professional we can be with our quotation letter, as this will lend credibility to us and our company and therefore increase the chances of the customer placing an order.

I know of one major company that goes to the time and trouble of reproducing its customer's logo and style of letterhead on the face page of the proposal. With binding machines and spiral binders being so inexpensive, it is simple enough to have covers printed specifically for your sales proposals. You could bind each one and present it in its best possible format to your customers.

5. If you're dealing in a situation where more than one person makes the decision concerning the purchase, send sufficient originals of the proposal.
6. Keep records. When we obtain an order and have built a relationship with our customer, we can go back to our ideas about finding out why people buy by asking for the customer's opinion of the sales quotations letter. By taking careful notes we will be able to change those items that need changing and keep those items that work in future letters.
7. Wherever possible, in my opinion, do not send your sales quotations letter via a fax machine. Information presented from many fax machines is very poor, and this cannot possibly enhance your quotation. Postal services are so efficient and courier costs so inexpensive that minimal time and expense are involved in ensuring our quality proposals land on our customers' desks in their best possible presentation.

CHAPTER 20

Neuro-linguistic programming

Neuro-linguistic programming (NLP) is a scientifically proved method of creating change in oneself. Developed in the early 1970s by Richard Bandler (an information scientist) and John Grinder, (a linguistics professor), NLP prompts us into examining our perception of the world: after all, our memory of an event may be totally different from another person's memory of the same event. Who is right? Both are.

What is important to us is *our* memory – that is all we have to recall. All our thoughts and deeds are based on our perception of the world, not on the world itself. When we understand how our thoughts and feelings are recorded in our minds, we have created an opportunity to change them.

NLP has been called 'software for the brain', the notion being that, if someone else can achieve something, then so can we. Bandler and Grinder examined sportsmen and women to find out if the top performers had anything in common. They did. NLP says that, if other people can do it, so can you.

I have been using NLP for a number of years and have found it enables me to make personal changes as well as build rapport with people in ways I never before thought possible. NLP is a practical method of changing the way we think and behave faster and more easily than ever before. It is based on a few simple but powerful ideas. If we change the way we think about an experience, we can change that experience for ourselves.

There isn't space here to consider all aspects of NLP; however, I can give you a taste of it and then, if you require further information, there is a variety of actions you can take.

We have already looked at how we can use NLP to build rapport at a subconscious level with other people by establishing people's 'home base' of language – be this visual, auditory or kinesthetic. Practise these ideas until they become second nature to you.

An additional technique we can use to find out about other people's home base of language at any particular moment is to watch their eyes. Imagine you've asked someone a question and, before answering, their eyes move upwards. They are probably accessing their information in the visual way. If their eyes move from side to side, towards their ears, they are accessing information in an auditory way. If their eyes move down, particularly towards their feeling hand, they're probably accessing information in a kinesthetic or feeling way. Spotting eye movements is as easy as spotting language once we're practised at it.

Let's now look at how we can use NLP to change ourselves and change our representations and memories of the world. Recall, if you will, a pleasurable experience. Bring it into your mind's eye. Try to see that picture (some people can see pictures easily) or perhaps hear what was going on in that experience. Even try to recall the feelings of that experience.

Now push that feeling away from you, make it dimmer, perhaps going into black and white if it was originally in colour. Give less volume to the sound, less intensity to the feelings: push it away from you. Now bring it back to where it was before. Bring it even closer so the sounds are louder, the picture bigger. Make it brighter, more colourful, the feelings more intense. I am sure you will feel the difference. Finally, push it back to where it was at the start and let go of it.

I'm sure this brief explanation will start to make us all understand how our minds relate to the experiences stored in our heads. Did you feel the differences when you were pushing that experience away and when you were pulling it closer to you? If you didn't, try it again. Push it away, bring it closer and then put it back where it was in your mind, in its original place before we started this discussion.

We can use this technique in a variety of ways. First, if we are having a problem with something, we could simply push it away and make it less intense, less loud, less visible to us. If there was a situation where we wanted to increase the intensity of the feeling – where we wanted to make it better for us – we could pull it in towards us so we could remember it in a more pleasurable way.

The way we could use NLP in public speaking for example, to get over our nerves, is as follows. Stand up. Go back in your mind, if you can, to a time when you were particularly confident – very, very confident. Take a moment to do this. Relive that moment, see what you were seeing, hear what you were hearing and feel what you were feeling.

As you feel that confidence building up inside you, imagine a coloured circle on the floor around your feet. Now step out of that circle leaving all those confident feelings inside the circle. This will seem peculiar or strange, but it works because your thoughts can move faster than your feelings. If you don't feel you've actually stepped out of the circle, step further back until you know you've definitely stepped out of it, leaving your feelings in it.

Think of a time in the future when you want to have those same feelings of confidence: perhaps the next time you're going to speak in public. See and hear what will be there, just before you want that confidence. Could it be the room in which you're going to speak or someone's office door? Whatever it is, with that thought in your mind, step back into the circle and feel all those confident feelings again.

I am sure you are already feeling better about the event to come and, when it arrives, you will find you have already pre-programmed yourself to respond in a more confident way. You are now deciding for yourself how you want to react to any particular situation.

This is called 'the circle of excellence'. I have used it and was extremely surprised how well it worked. At first I was sceptical, thinking it unlikely to work. However, I tried it. I can remember the situation now. I had made the future triggering event getting out of my car. Sure enough, when I arrived at a particular speaking engagement and got out of the car, there in my mind on the ground was that circle of excellence, and all those confident feelings came flooding back.

Another way NLP can make us more successful in our lives is as follows. If we are able to find our own switches, the switches that trigger us into certain types of activity, we are able to switch that switch and trigger the feeling whenever we want it.

For example, think of a feeling now that you'd like to recreate at some time. This might be confidence, happiness, etc. Whatever it is, get that feeling back into your body now. For the sake of discussion we'll call it 'A'. Notice the changes in you compared to how you were feeling a few moments ago. Is your breathing different? Is your posture different? Are you sitting differently? Is your head in a different position? Look at all parts of your body and decide what the differences are.

Now change from that particular feeling and go into a different feeling, 'B'. This might be the feeling you were in to start with. Note the differences, note all the differences in your body. Now back into A. See the changes again. You now know what the switches are that change you from B to A. You've found your own switches. In order to feel A, you have to do the things you do when you are in state A.

There are many ways you can use this for so many different feelings – at any time *you* like. It's rather like having a menu of feelings. You select the one you want at any moment, trigger it by knowing the changes that make it happen and, bingo, there it is!

Another way we can use NLP arises from the research done by Anthony Robbins and his ideas of anchoring a particular feeling to a particular physical touch. For example, take a situation where you are feeling extremely happy and, at the moment of that intense feeling, pinch your wrist. What you have done is to anchor that happy feeling to a pinch on the wrist. If you pinch your wrist again you'll trigger back that happy feeling.

I'm certain that, if you give this some thought after reading this chapter, you'll realise there are many triggers in your life that already create specific feelings within you: perhaps a particular smell, a particular sound or a particular song. Most certainly, particular touches bring all sorts of different feelings that have been anchored in the past.

This is sufficient as an introduction to NLP, which would need three or four weeks of seminars or five or six books to explain in full.

CHAPTER 21

Peak performance

We are now going to discuss peak performance: how we can use all those skills we've discussed and get them into action to increase our success. I recently read the following by Michael Landon: 'Someone should tell us right at the start of our lives that we are dying. Then we might live life to the limit. Every minute of every day, "Do it!" I say "Do it now!", there are only so many tomorrows.'

We have discussed taking action before, and how the actual 'taking' of the action is easy but how the 'deciding' is the key. Remember the warm bed and the cold room (Chapter 2)? We have to take some time to decide, and decide categorically and firmly that we will take the actions concerned to make us more successful. Sometimes our decision-making computer program in our minds is a bit rusty.

Let's keep practising with it so we can get it well oiled and used to making fast decisions. It's always said that successful people make decisions quickly and change their minds slowly, and that unsuccessful people make decisions slowly but change their minds quickly.

We all get a choice in life as to which road we tread, and I'm reminded of that excellent film, *Parenthood,* starring the comedy-actor, Steve Martin. Towards the end of the film Martin is sitting in his kitchen with his wife. He's just lost his job and she's found out she's pregnant again – an unplanned pregnancy. The old granny in the film comes in and sees the pair of them looking downhearted. She says: 'When I first went out with the man who was later to become my husband, he took me to the fair and said to me "Do you want to go on the merry-go-round or on the roller coaster?" I said I'd rather go on the roller coaster because although it was going to be a scary ride with ups and downs, it was certainly going to be more fun than on the merry-go-round.' She then left the kitchen to go and sit in the car to wait for Martin and his wife.

Martin's wife turned to him and said: 'You do realise she was talking about life, don't you?'

Isn't it true that we all do get a choice of whether we go on the roller coaster or the merry-go-round – the safe round and round – or the exhilarating but risky roller coaster of life?

To achieve our peak performance we need to undertake a variety of basic actions. First, we need to set goals. Second, we need to use the techniques used by advertising companies to sell us their products. What do they use? Pain and pleasure: the pain we will avoid by taking action and the pleasure we will gain by taking action.

If you think of all the advertisements that motivate us to buy, this is exactly how it's done. Let's use those same ideas, the pain and pleasure statements, to motivate ourselves into action.

Think of it like this. Imagine you were sitting on a see-saw at the lower end. How much weight would we need to *slam* on the other end of the see-saw to galvanise you into action? Only you know!

In your mind's eye you could construct a box, a large wooden box, and into that box you could put reason after reason after reason for pain and pleasure, each one weighing heavier than the one before it; until the box was so full and so heavy you had to get a team of people to lift it to *slam* it on the other side of the see-saw, thereby catapulting you to your peak performance.

As we have been discussing the sales business, what we need are some heavy reasons why we need to do sales calls. (Obviously, you can use this method for any other actions you want to take.) But for the example of selling, in a few minutes I want you to write down ten pain reasons why you must do sales calls and ten pleasure reasons why you must do them. Could some of them be the following?

Pain
No commission
No job
No car
No money
No home
No holiday
No drinks
No meals
No wife/husband
No kids
No pleasure

Pleasure
Great job
High self-esteem
High self-confidence
Lots of holidays
Great home
Fantastic lifestyle
Total security

Peace of mind
High reputation
Love

What I'd like you to do now is fill in the following, saying why you know you must do sales calls:

Pain

1. ____________________
2. ____________________
3. ____________________
4. ____________________
5. ____________________
6. ____________________
7. ____________________
8. ____________________
9. ____________________
10. ____________________

Pleasure

1. ____________________
2. ____________________
3. ____________________
4. ____________________
5. ____________________
6. ____________________
7. ____________________
8. ____________________
9. ____________________
10. ____________________

Another way to ensure our peak performance is to be perfectly prepared to make mistakes. As with goal setting it is always said that the people who *don't* make mistakes end up working for the people who do make mistakes.

Be prepared for the mistakes so that we can learn from them; after all, there are no failures in life, only results. We've looked at a variety of ways to establish the actions we need to take – for example, preview/review and windows of opportunity. We can use the windows of opportunity for our commercial and private lives.

We must ensure we have our personal finances in order: that we only spend the profit and never the cash flow so we're not left with too much month at the end of the money.

The only way we're ever going to learn to swim is in the water. We can learn all the ideas on the side of the baths, but we still need to get in the water to start really learning to swim. It's exactly the same with selling: you've got to go out and sell. Practice will help but in the end you have to go out there and do it.

A way we can improve our chances for success and our abilities to increase the actions we take is to let go of yesterday. Are there things that have happened in your life, up to now, that you regret? Fine, we all have them. Let go of them. If there are people you feel you should apologise to, go and apologise to them. If there are people you're angry with, forgive them. Let go of yesterday; you can never live there again.

The reason most people don't buy the clothes they want is that they don't have the space in their wardrobes to put them. Often it's the same with people's minds. Let's make sure we clear out our wardrobes and give away the clothes that will never fit again so that we've the space for some new clothes. Similarly with our minds, let go of yesterday, of yesterday's problems, of yesterday's anger to make space for tomorrow's pleasure.

It's said that when the Vikings attacked a new country the commander would burn the boats when they'd landed on the foreign shore. Why? Because that way he'd ensure everyone knew there was no way back and therefore the only way was forward.

I'm always amazed when I hear people say they had better have a 'fall-back' position, that we ought to have a 'proper job' to go back to if our sales career doesn't work. I'm sure you've noticed that those people with fall-back positions usually fall back to them. Those people who have only one choice of direction, namely forwards, end up going forward. It's a hard-line position, but burn those boats, burn those bridges and then you've no choice but to take the actions you need to take.

I also believe that peak performance is determined by our attitude. We discussed earlier how the only thing that was important in sales success was attitude. No other factors have ever been proved to have such a major impact. Let's make sure we've got our attitude right, that the computer programs in our minds are saying: 'I always remember people's names', 'As I get older, my memory gets better,' 'I am always confident', 'I can always do something new', 'I always have time in my life.'

We need to sell ourselves on ourselves and, if you ever have difficulty doing this, use another neuro-linguistic programming technique called 'seeing yourself through the eyes of love'. Visualise yourself in the way someone else would visualise you, a person who loves you. You see only the good parts, only the good attitude.

Use paper. I think it is a good idea to write questions to yourself. Then answer them . . . in writing. The very act of committing your thoughts to paper sometimes seems to make them come true. Using paper doesn't *waste* time, it uses time effectively.

The steps to success

Step 1

Make a decision to be successful. Write it on a piece of paper, sign it and date it.

Step 2

Write down ten reasons, using pain, why you must make sales calls or must take the actions relevant to your success.

Step 3

Write down ten reasons, for pleasure, why you must take the actions relevant to your success.

Step 4

Write a slogan or advertising jingle to advertise you and your success to you.

Step 5

Take the necessary actions to let go of the past.

Step 6

Make sure you have put in a reward system for yourself for the stops along the way. After all, success is a journey . . . not a destination.

CHAPTER 22

Finale

Before I tell you the story of the two frogs, there's a couple of things we need to do. First, we need to re-do our self-assessment test (and we need to do it in two different ways) and give ourselves a mark out of ten, in response to each answer, as to our current skill or ability level.

Second, we need to reassess our starting point as it was before reading this book. What I'd like you to do is answer each question a second time, giving yourself a mark out of ten for where you really believe you started now that we have discussed all the various topics.

Key areas for success in selling

We have discussed a great range of topics, namely:

Active listening

How we can learn so much just by talking that little bit less and listening that little bit more.

Positive attitude

Dealing with everyone with enthusiasm. Living by the rule that there are no failures in life, only results.

Avoiding procrastination

Using the salami principle to slice our tasks into bite-sized pieces and then polishing them off just one at a time.

Why people buy

Finding out why we buy and why our customers buy so we can tailor our approach and content to ensure our customers benefit.

Remember, our success is only a by-product of our customers' success.

Open and closed questions

We discussed questioning and how powerful questions can be.

Power communications

What we say, 'Did you do Latin?', how we say what we say, the way in which we use our voices for maximum effect and, of course, that fascinating topic . . .

Body language

This really is the unspoken truth. We looked (see how visual I am) at reading the customer's eyes and how much we could learn by simply watching actively.

Opening statements

Now we have a new effective opening to our sales conversations, we are guaranteed to get more interviews and therefore more sales.

Features and benefits

How we can help the customer avoid all that hard mental work of translating the features of our product by using the simple expression, 'and that means to you . . .'

Translating objections

We now welcome customers' so-called objections. We interpret them as positive questions and reply accordingly.

The art of closing

We covered 25 ways in which we could help our customers buy what they wanted to buy. How, by carefully using the closes, we could take away all the pressure from the sale and yet sell more and more.

Negotiation

If we have, on average, 40 years left in our lives and, with inflation, our average earnings over that period could be, say, £50,000, we will have received and probably spent £2 million.

Saving just 10 per cent by skilful use of the ideas we have discussed could save you £200,000. Just think what you could do with that.

Goal setting

The panacea for all our ills, the cure-all for our troubles, the key skill for all successful people. Take the time to set your goals – it will be some of the best time you ever spent.

Creative action

We examined and played with six different ways in which we could be creative. Your answers to the paper-clip quiz proved how creative you already are. Use this creativity!

Time management

Time, our most valuable asset. Remember the tramp? 'There but for *me* go I.'

Use preview/review, spend time planning, get your life organised and you will have increased dramatically your chances for success.

Telephone techniques

We discussed a variety of ideas to get past the 'rejectionists' and how, by some simple pre-planning, we can capitalise on the use of the phone.

Keeping records

All of us should prepare our windows of opportunity chart so we can see clearly where sales will come from easily in the months and years ahead.

Rejection analysis

I am certain that, if we analyse our strengths as well as our weaknesses, and take action to maintain and improve . . . nothing can stop us succeeding!

Image

Remember . . . the book by the cover. We *never* get a second chance to make a first impression. Let's act like professionals, think like professionals and dress as the professionals we are.

Writing sales letters

You now have some proven methods to design and run a mail-shot campaign.

Sales quotations letters will, if you use the ideas we've discussed, be a selling aid and not a sales prevention.

NLP

I find neuro-linguistic programming a fascinating subject. I suggest you use the 'circle of excellence' on a regular basis. If you want further information about NLP, write to me care of the publishers and I'll send it to you.

Peak performance

We now know where our action switch is located and, more importantly, how to press it.

All the knowledge in the world is of little use unless we do something with it. It's not what we know but what we do with what we know that counts. Let me finish by sharing with you the story of the two frogs.

Once upon a time there were two frogs

Once upon a time there were two frogs, who were hopping about in a farmer's yard. In the yard they spied a bucket full of milk. They hopped over to the bucket, jumped in and drank all the milk. They lay down in the bottom of the bucket, happy and bloated.

Suddenly a crowd of frogs came round, jumping and hopping and shouting: 'You'd better get out of there! The farmer's coming and he's going to get you!'

So the frogs in the bucket started to jump and jump. Unfortunately, because they'd drunk so much milk, they couldn't jump out of the bucket. They tried and tried. The crowd of frogs jeered at them, telling them they would fail, that they couldn't jump out of the bucket, and that the farmer was going to get them.

Still they tried until, finally, one of the frogs gave up and fell to the bottom of the bucket . . . defeated.

The other frog kept on jumping, and still the crowd jeered at him, telling him he wouldn't do it. The farmer would get him, he would fail. But he kept on jumping until finally he jumped right out of the bucket and got away.

How did he manage to succeed with all that negativity going on around him, with all those frogs telling him he would fail?

I'll tell you . . .

He Was Deaf

He thought they were cheering . . . *not* jeering.

How many times in our lives do we need to be deaf, do we need to *stop* believing all those negative people who tell us we will fail, when we know inside we do have *the will to win?*

If you define your success, if you blend the ideas discussed in this book with your own thoughts and skills, and if you take ACTION, then your success . . .*is guaranteed.*

Further reading

Buzan, Tony: *Make the Most of Your Mind,* Pan
Master Your Memory, David and Charles
Speed Memory, David and Charles
Use Your Head, BBC
Use Your Memory, BBC

Dimke, Dan Lee: *The Mega Strategy*, Billion Books, Future World Co, Dallas

Kennedy, Gavin: *Everything is Negotiable,* Arrow

Books from Kogan Page

Auer, J T: *Inspired Selling: A Book of Ideas, Opportunities and Renewal*

Denny, Richard: *Selling to Win: Tested Techniques for Closing the Sale*

Golis, Christoper C: *Empathy Selling: The Powerful New Technique for the 1990s*

Ley D Forbes: *The Best Seller*

Mercer, David: *The Sales Professional: Strategies and Techniques for Managing the High-level Sale*

Schiffman, Stephan: *Cold Calling Techniques*
The 25 Most Common Sales Mistakes . . . and How to Avoid Them

Tirbutt, Edmund: *How to Increase Sales Without Leaving Your Desk*

A full list is available from the publisher.

Index

References in italics indicate figures or tables.

Also by Peter Thomson

If you have enjoyed *Sell Your Way to the Top* and have found it of benefit, please send for details of the other services by Peter Thomson.

AUDIO TAPES
- Selling ☐
- Personal Development ☐
- Entrepreneurial Skills ☐
- Management Skills ☐
- Public Speaking ☐

OPEN SEMINARS
- Selling ☐
- Personal Development ☐
- Entrepreneurial Skills ☐
- Management Skills ☐
- Public Speaking ☐

IN-HOUSE SALES & PERSONAL
DEVELOPMENT SEMINARS ☐

Return this page or a photocopy of it to:

PINNACLE DEVELOPMENT TRAINING LTD
20–22 High Street, Birmingham B14 7JU
Tel: 021-441 5411 Fax: 021-441 5400